Ask the
bird
Keeper

MARC MORRONE
with Amy Fernandez

To Harry,
the bird I didn't give up at gunpoint

Original illustrations © 2009 by Jason O'Malley. Photographs © 2009 by Cioli/Hunnicutt
BowTie Studio, Isabelle Français, Daniel Maldonado (www.canarysave.com),
Argiris Savopoulos (greekfancypigeons.com), Dennis Soares, Dan Voydanoff
(www.voydanoff.net), and Shutterstock.com.

Library of Congress Cataloging-in-Publication Data

Morrone, Marc, 1960-
 [Ask the bird keeper]
 Marc Morrone's ask the bird keeper / by Marc Morrone with Amy Fernandez.
    p. cm.
 ISBN 978-1-933958-31-6
1. Cage birds—Miscellanea. 2. Cage birds—Health—Miscellanea. 3. Cage birds—
Behavior—Miscellanea. I. Fernandez, Amy. II. Title. III. Title: Ask the bird keeper.
 SF461.M69 2009
 636.6—dc22
                                    2009009828

BowTie Press®
A Division of BowTie, Inc.
3 Burroughs
Irvine, California 92618

Printed and bound in Singapore
16 15 14 13 12 11 10 09   1 2 3 4 5 6 7 8 9 10

CONTENTS

FOREWORD

BY MARTHA STEWART

I got my first birds while a student at Barnard College. My husband and I were living in a three-room apartment on West 114th Street that had no view except one of cluttered rooftops and smoke-emitting incinerator chimneys.

We bought two bluish parakeets who sang for us all day, lived in a spacious cage, and taught me so much about the complex and wonderful life of birds. Aetheltwig and Aethelred were friendly, intelligent, and always looking for a way to escape confinement. They were free whenever we were home—they flew around the small apartment, sat on my pen as I wrote my college papers, perched on the moving carriage of my electric typewriter, and ate my cornflakes or raisin bran while sitting on the edge of my breakfast bowl.

They seemed to be busy all day long—eating, bathing, singing, squawking, or playing with things. They were so much fun. One day, they did get the opportunity to be free. A small, expandable screen fell out of one of the slightly open windows, leaving just enough space for them to wiggle their way, unobserved, to the great outdoors. They did not return, and I was heartbroken.

My next bird was given to me by my husband as a replacement for his company (we were divorcing). José Arcadio Buendía (named after a character from *One Hundred Years of Solitude* by Gabriel García Márquez) was a conure, and if my husband had researched the species, he would have known that conures are long lived, the noisiest of birds, extremely demanding of attention, and destructive—and this one was a jewelry thief as well. I had five years with José before a friend fell in love with him and offered to adopt him.

I always wanted a cockatoo or big parrot after José, but I realized the gigantic responsibility such a bird represented, and I have settled for an ever-expanding group of red canaries who enliven my home daily with beautiful song, constant rustling noises, and colorful activity.

And who is my bird mentor, my coach, my teacher, and my guide? Marc Morrone, of course. He is so knowledgeable and so practical in his approach to the care of all birds. I can always count on Marc's years of experience to help me solve my problems and deal with my challenges in handling my flock on a daily basis. As a result of his intelligent and sensible advice, I could not be happier or more at ease raising and keeping my healthy and growing collection.

Thanks, Marc!

—Martha Stewart, April 2009

INTRODUCTION

One of my favorite books is George Orwell's *Animal Farm.* In this story, a bunch of farm animals get together, kick the humans off the farm, and decide to run it themselves. At first, the animals posted a bill of rights on the wall of the barn, proclaiming that all animals were equal, all humans were bad, and so forth. As time went on, some of the animals cleverly manipulated the others into doing all of the work and began treating them as commodities, just like the human farmers did. At the end, the pigs start wearing clothes, walking upright, and buying and selling the other animals. To the other animals' astonishment, they find a new slogan on the barn wall, saying that all animals are equal but some are more equal than others. This is pretty much the way many humans view birds; with the exception of a few endangered species such as whooping cranes, all birds are legally defined as commodities. We can use them as we wish as long as it's done in a humane manner.

These uses vary considerably, from outright cruelty toward chickens and turkeys to extreme adulation for parrots and canaries. Cruelty is justified by claiming that particular

birds are not intelligent or worthy of compassion and humane care. In reality, its defenders are trying to rationalize inhumane treatment. But realistically, what's the difference between a pigeon, a chicken, a parakeet, and a canary? Why do we justify eating some birds, and would never consider keeping them as pets, while other birds are coddled and spoiled as clever companions?

I find all birds equally fascinating and feel that they all deserve the same level of care. If chickens, pheasants, turkeys, ducks, geese, and quail are important food sources, then that's the way of the world. But the fact that we eat them doesn't mean they don't deserve a happy life and a humane death. Laws should ensure humane care of birds used for food. If we must pay an extra dollar a pound for chicken cutlets in order to give these birds a decent quality of life, then that is the price we should pay to consume another sentient being. And birds are no less sentient than dogs or cats. In some ways, they are even more intelligent. They all can make great pets, and I have developed great relationships with birds ranging from ostriches to hummingbirds.

This book is one of few that present all species of birds as potential pets and animals equally receptive to a relationship with humans. Some may think that parrots are the best pet birds, but they aren't ideal for everyone. You can interact well with a finch, canary, pigeon, or duck. Parrots have simply had better publicity because of their ability to mimic human words. (I'm sure that the first parrot that ever did that would have regretted it if he'd known how that little "trick" would be exploited in centuries to come—besides, parrots have far more to offer than conversation.)

All birds are fascinating. A bird's beak, feathers, upright stance, eyes, and song—it's simply amazing that a creature so physically different from us exists on this planet, and in studying bird anatomy, it is easy to see evidence of the bird's prehistoric ancestors: When bird owners complain to me that their bird doesn't want to be touched, or it makes too much noise, or it chews on furniture, I have to roll my eyes. I really want to ask them why they cannot appreciate this magnificent creature sharing their living space, but what I settle for is simply answering their questions, which is what I am going to do in this book.

An Apple a Day

Birds will basically eat anything if they are regularly exposed to it, but they are highly individualistic about the fruits and vegetables they eat. My birds eat absolutely any fruit or vegetable except for strawberries. These are strawberries that I worked hard to grow, from my backyard, and which are eaten ravenously by wild birds. I have no idea why my pet birds do not like them. As a general rule, birds don't like soft, juicy fruits or vegetables like peaches, plums, and bananas. They prefer crisp textures like apples, pomegranates, string beans, and carrots. But I also have birds that love bananas. Birds can eat any fruits and vegetables except for avocados, which can be poisonous to some birds and could even cause death.

Twice a week, the greengrocer makes a delivery to my store with every type of fruit and vegetable that he has available. We cut these up and feed some to all of the birds every day: canaries, doves, pigeons, and so forth. The only birds that don't get these treats are my falcons, owls, and eagles. If you aren't able to do this for your bird, you can get a bag of frozen mixed garden vegetables. Thaw them out and keep them in the refrigerator in a plastic container. Mix them with canned fruit cocktail packed in juice, not syrup. Sprinkle a pinch of vitamin supplement on top to replace the vitamins lost in processing, and give your bird a dish of this mixture every day. Admittedly, this is not as good as giving the bird fresh produce every day, but it's better than feeding the bird only dry seeds and pellets. It takes no time to prepare this, and it greatly improves your bird's diet.

If your bird is terrified of trying new fruits and vegetables, rather than giving him grapes or plums, try something hard and crispy. It may also help to serve new things in a more interesting way. Birds love grabbing things. Those skewer toys, which are really just kabob sticks, are perfect for this. Cut up crispy things like apples, sweet potatoes, celery, and carrots, impale them on the stick, and hang the stick in the bird's cage. He will grab the fruit and vegetable pieces and chew them for amusement.

If you are creative and persistent, your bird will eventually acquire a taste for fruits and vegetables, but he must make this decision. There is no way you can persuade him to experiment with new foods if he doesn't want to.

What is the best diet for baby chicks?

In nature, baby chicks, pheasants, and quails are omnivorous. They dart around, eating insects, seeds, and greens. Commercially made starter mashes have the right balance of fat, protein, and carbohydrates. As the chick grows, this should be adjusted based on what the chicken will do for a living. A hen that lays eggs needs a different pellet formula because egg-laying birds need extra calcium and protein. Most feed and grain stores stock the appropriate growing mashes and laying pellets for chickens. It is important to use a commercial formula rather than a homemade diet because the latter will not contain the proper balance of nutrients. Your chick may end up with a crooked bill or crooked legs as a result. If bone growth starts off wrong, it cannot be corrected later.

Is it OK to make my own homemade bird food from grains I buy at the health food store? Is this better for my bird?

If organic grains are better for you, of course they would be better for your bird. As long as the diet is properly balanced, there is nothing wrong with this. But if you have lots of birds like I do, it can be very hard to make your own bird food. Homemade pet food, for any pet, is always preferable to commercial pet foods. Again, this also depends on the time and money you have available. Give the bird the largest variety of grains that you can provide, but remember that this only constitutes part of a balanced diet. Fresh fruits and vegetables are equally important. When it comes to pet keeping, balance is the key—for both environment and diet.

How do dietary changes affect the appearance of a bird's droppings?

Birds have a very fast metabolism, so whatever goes in comes out right away. That's why they poop so much. If your bird eats carrots or red peppers, they will show up right away in his droppings. As a general rule, the color of a bird's stool will vary based on what it has eaten. However, the color of the urates, the white part of the droppings, should always be white. Excess water in the bird's system will be excreted as clear water. If the bird is healthy, the droppings should be distinctly separate no matter what it ingests. The water should be clear, the urates should be white, and the stool should have some consistency regardless of color. If any one of these is compromised, such as the stool being liquid or the urine being yellow, you know that there is something wrong with the bird and you should visit your vet immediately.

How often should I give my finches fruit or greens? Sometimes they never touch them. They really don't seem crazy about them.

Canaries are finches, and they go crazy for fruit and greens. Some finches, such as bronze-wing manikins and tricolor nuns, don't like them as much. However, very often, if one finch starts eating the greens, the rest of the birds will try them. They have a herd mentality. Mainly, it's a matter of offering greens to them consistently in an attractive way. You can buy 4" x 6" wire shelves that hook onto the side of the birdcage. Finches like to sit on these little platforms. If you place some cut-up fruit and greens on the shelves, the bird will be surrounded when sitting there. Out of curiosity, he will sample the food. Since finches are uncomfortable sitting on the bottom of the cage, the birds are less likely to investigate food placed there. The birds are more relaxed sitting on the cage shelves, and thus are more likely to try something new.

Is tap water safe for my birds?

If you don't drink your tap water, it's probably not safe for your birds, either. Some people will counter this, saying that outdoor birds drink from puddles. But those birds choose to drink from those puddles. If something is not quite right with the puddle water, they will fly to another source. You have to make a decision based on the tap water quality in your area.

What are the best dishes to get for my parrots? These birds either tip their dishes over or chew them up.

Parrots are curious animals, and they like to manipulate things. Animals have no concept of the future. Your bird has no idea that tipping over his food dish means he will have no food for later on. He lives in the moment. If he has fun tipping over his dish, he sees no reason not to do it. Further, parrots in the wild spend the entire day looking for food, and much of the food they find are nuts encased in hard shells. It takes them a long time to chew through these shells. As a result, many pet parrots have unfulfilled chewing desires. They need an outlet for their desire to chew just as dogs do.

The solution is to buy dishes with locks. That solves the tipping problem, but the birds still need something to manipulate and chew. That's why we put toys in the birdcage. Many people think it's pointless to put toys in the birdcage because the birds chew them up—but that's what they are for. If you don't provide things for them to chew, your birds will turn to their perches or, worse, their feathers. And once a bird starts chewing his feathers, it's very hard to get him to stop.

What is the best way to add extra protein to my bird's diet?

What makes you think your bird needs extra protein? The only time a bird needs this is when expending extra energy flying or breeding. Most pet birds do neither. In nature, canaries eat only seeds. However, during their breeding season, they will eat insects because they need extra protein. To compensate for this, most canary breeders give their birds egg food: crumbled hard-boiled eggs mixed with a couple of other ingredients. A hard-boiled egg is one of the best sources of protein; however, some psittacines crave raw meat. Mine love it, and I use raw chopped meat for a training reward when teaching them to fly to me on command. They love this more than anything. My African Grey, Darwin, and my hyacinth macaw, Remus, will do anything for raw chopped meat. When clutching a piece of raw meat in his foot, chomping away at it, Remus looks more evil and sinister than any bird of prey I've ever owned. But I don't give them chopped meat on a daily basis because, in nature, when would a parrot be eating a raw cow? When feeding birds, their diet should closely resemble what their wild relatives would normally consume. Check with your avain veterinarian before feeding raw meat.

What is the deal with grit? I always thought that all birds need this, but I also heard that eating grit can kill my bird.

Like anything else in life, too much of a good thing is bad. Traditionally, birds that need grit are species that swallow whole grains, such as pigeons, doves, chickens, and pheasants. If a bird swallows a pea, sunflower seed, or corn kernel, it needs to be masticated in some way since birds don't have teeth. It first goes to the crop, where it is softened by digestive juices, and then to the gizzard, which contains the grit and gravel the bird has eaten. This is where the seeds are ground up. In nature, birds eat just enough grit and gravel to aid digestion. Birds in captivity may eat excessive amounts of grit and gravel if it is always available and they have nothing else to do. As a result, their gizzards become impacted with grit, which can cause serious problems.

Parrots, parakeets, canaries, and finches remove the shells from their seeds and chew them in their bills before swallowing. These birds really don't need grit, but they do like a little every now and then. But if they have it available all the time, they will definitely eat more than they need, especially since they really don't need it at all. Either ration the grit carefully, or don't bother giving it. I only give it to my birds that swallow seeds whole.

Does my bird need vitamin supplements?

In a perfect world, birds would not need supplements. But birds that are kept indoors and not exposed to natural light are always compromised in one way or another. I've always added vitamin supplements to my birds' diets. There are so many available, in powdered and liquid forms. The only birds that don't need them are birds kept outdoors with daily exposure to natural light. (But I still add calcium supplements to their food.) It seems that every bird needs something. There is a bird of prey kept by falconers called the Harris's hawk (pictured). Its natural habitat is the deserts of Texas and Arizona. When they are kept by falconers in colder regions such as the Northeast, their bones become brittle unless they get a daily calcium supplement. This happens even though these birds are kept outdoors and fed the same natural diet of rodents and birds that they would normally consume in Texas and Arizona. The difference is that they are exposed to much more natural sunlight in the Southwest. In a natural situation, they would never live this far north, where the natural sunlight is insufficient for them to synthesize calcium from their diet to maintain bone strength.

What table foods can I share with my bird? I've seen people feeding birds pizza, chocolate cake, and hot dogs. Is this OK?

A diet of hot dogs and pizza is not healthy for anybody, but an occasional piece of pizza is fine. The same applies to birds. Like us, they are social animals and like to eat in groups. If your bird sees you eating something and wants a taste, there is nothing wrong with it as long as this is an occasional treat, rather than a mainstay of the bird's diet. Common sense rules.

As a general rule, I would avoid giving birds caffeine products (including chocolate, which can be toxic) and alcohol. No drunken birds needed—they are crazy enough as it is. And they are wired enough without caffeine.

How can I tell if my bird is getting too fat? He seems to eat all day long.

Most birds that are kept as pets are too fat because they do eat all day and rarely get enough exercise. However, a bird that eats mostly high-fat foods such as sunflower seeds will be a lot fatter than a bird that also eats pellets, fruits, and vegetables. Monitor your bird's diet and make sure he is eating a healthy variety. In nature, birds normally do eat all day long, but they don't necessarily eat the same thing. Make sure that your bird doesn't consume a diet of exclusively high-fat foods and give him as much exercise as possible. If your bird's wing feathers are trimmed and he can't fly, he can still do bird aerobics: hold him on your hand and move it up and down so that he flaps his wings hard.

It also helps to have a bird scale. This is a gram scale with a little perch, and birds quickly learn to step on the perch. Weigh him weekly to check if he is gaining or losing weight. If the number goes up or down dramatically, you know it's time to check in with your avian vet. By keeping an accurate log book, you can be proactive in determining if he has a budding weight problem. Birds that are working in bird shows must be at their ideal weight to fly properly and are weighed daily. This is known as the bird's flying weight, and you must know precisely how much food to give the bird each day to keep it at optimum flying weight. Birds kept at cooler temperatures need more food to maintain their flying weight compared with birds kept at warmer temperatures.

How do I convert my bird to a pelleted diet?

This causes a lot of stress for people because they don't understand how a bird's mind works. Except for a few species like snail kites (pictured opposite page), which only eat one type of snail, most pet birds are opportunistic feeders.

They will experiment with just about anything. When I was in South America, I remember watching the conures and Amazons walking about the streets like pigeons, scavenging any scraps they could find from sidewalk cracks. This is a perfect example of hunger being the best sauce. These birds were starving and would have eaten any organic material they found. I'm not recommending starving your bird, but the key may be to not give him quite so many choices.

If your bird has been eating seed for a number of years, he is probably hooked on this diet. The easiest way to convert him to eating pellets, fruits, and vegetables is to put dishes of these foods in his cage each morning—no seeds at all. He will probably look at these new foods in horror and glare at you. Forget about it and go to work. When you come home, you will probably find this food uneaten or scattered around the cage.

Offer him a dish of seeds and let him eat his fill for half an hour. Then take away all of the food until the next morning, when you give him new servings of pellets, fruits, and vegetables. The bird is not being starved. Allowing him to eat his fill of seeds for half an hour is plenty of time for him to fill his crop and not go to bed hungry. When he gets up in the morning, he will have a good appetite, though, and will look forward to whatever you give him. But he will still probably glare at you when you give him his new breakfast and be furiously pacing around when you get home at night. When you serve his dinner of seeds, he will probably consume them ravenously until you take them away in half an hour.

Just keep doing this. He will wake up every morning with a good appetite and see you put those pellets in his cage. Eventually, out of sheer boredom, one day he will pick up a pellet and start chewing on it. This is comparable to someone on a diet who begrudgingly starts eating his carrot and celery sticks because they are hungry and bored and have no other foods available.

What is the best way to store my birdseed? It's a lot cheaper to buy a lot at once.

The best way to store birdseed is to keep it cold. Most birdseed comes complete with miller moth larvae or eggs of seed weevils, and when it is

kept at room temperature, these eggs eventually hatch. The weevils lay even more eggs. After about a month, you will open up the container of birdseed and discover more weevils than seeds. In addition, the miller moth larvae will turn into moths, which will fly all over your house and lay eggs in any grain products in your pantry.

If you keep your birdseed in a freezer, it will basically last until doomsday. Some people don't like to give their birds frozen seed, but it warms up within seconds, so this really isn't a big issue. If you buy seed in bulk in the wintertime, you can keep it in the trunk of your car. It will stay nice and cold, but this won't work in the summer unless you want a trunk full of moths.

What is seed testing? Do I need to do this?

In order to have full nutritional value, seeds must be alive. But it is pretty hard to know this just by looking at a seed, because it is dormant. Seed testing is a way to make this determination. Take some of your birdseed and spread it on a moist paper towel. If it is kept moist, at room temperature, these seeds should germinate in three days. At least 90 percent should germinate.

My canary loves to eat soaked seeds. Is this OK for him? How often is it safe to give this to him?

When the seeds germinate, all sorts of beneficial nutrients surge through them. This is known as soaked, germinated, or sprouted seed, and it is one of the most nutritious things you can feed your bird. There are many ways to make soaked seeds for birds and many products to do this. Any seed-eating bird will benefit from eating sprouted seed. I highly recommend that anyone who keeps birds invest in a seed sprouter so that you can easily give your birds sprouted seeds for a treat. In nature, birds always prefer sprouted seed. If you want to give this to your bird every day, it's fine. He will love it.

Is expensive birdseed really necessary? What's the difference? Doesn't it all really come from the same place?

Seeds may come from the same place but come from different plants. Wild birdseed mixes are very cheap, but they contain buckwheat, milo, and large millet, which most pet birds will not eat. Premium seed mixes contain safflower seeds, peas, and other more wholesome seeds. It is more expensive to grow safflower plants than to grow buckwheat plants, which explains the price difference. When I was a child, I could not afford premium seed mixes for my birds, so I gave them wild birdseed mixes supplemented with turkey pellets and as many fruits and vegetables as I could beg from the local greengrocer. My birds had a varied diet even though I was using cheaper food.

Pigeons seem to thrive on just about any kind of food and live just about everywhere. Is this some kind of superbird?

Pigeons live in cities mainly because cities are similar to their natural habitat. Pigeons evolved to live on cliffs and nest in nooks and crannies. All cities are full of food, and most birds could survive on the foods that pigeons find in cities. The major problem for birds in cities is the scarcity of suitable nesting sites. About the only birds that can find suitable nesting sites in cities are pigeons, starlings, English sparrows, and peregrine falcons, the latter of which nest on flat ledges of buildings and eat the other three birds. It's not necessarily that pigeons are so much more adaptable than other birds. They do well because the habitat in cities allows them to thrive. Song sparrows nest in low bushes on the ground and cannot survive in cities, although their diet is basically the same as that of English sparrows, which do very well in cities. English sparrows can find nesting areas in cities, but song sparrows cannot.

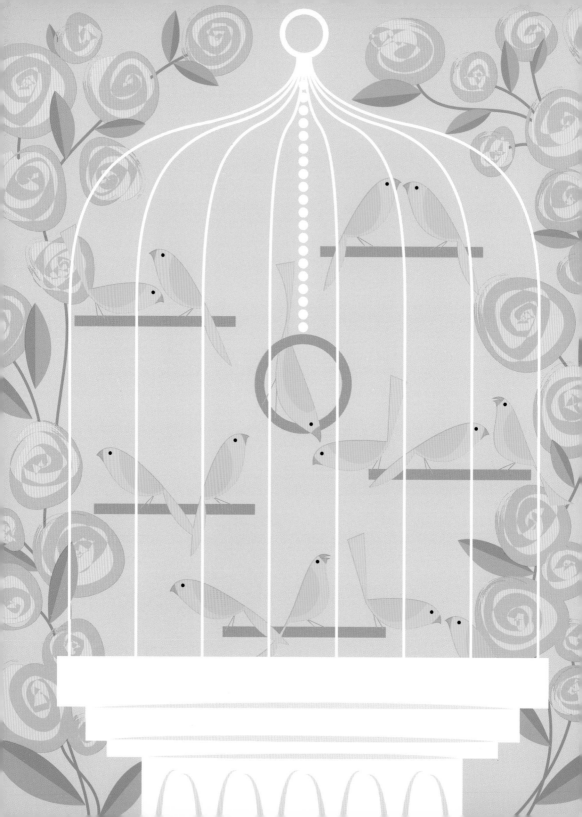

A Martha Stewart Home for Birds

Martha Stewart is an animal lover extraordinaire, and among her animals are birds. Her three favorite birds begin with the letter *C*. Her favorite pet bird is a Moluccan cockatoo by the name of Coral Ann. I've lived with Coral Ann for over twenty years, but this is just a working relationship. Coral Ann's heart belongs to Martha and no one else. When Coral Ann sees Martha, she gets all excited and starts talking and fluffing her crest feathers. She puts on a wonderful show. Unfortunately, this has never been televised, even though Coral Ann has been on television more than any other bird in the world. By the time the cameras start rolling, she has calmed down and contentedly sits on Martha's shoulder for the rest of the show. This has been a great source of frustration for Martha because she wants her fans to see Coral Ann's beautiful greeting display. But so far, in the ten years that the three of us have worked together, we've yet to time this display so that the TV cameras can catch it.

Absolutely nothing bothers Coral Ann. She sits on Martha's shoulder on live TV despite the distractions of music, clapping, dogs running around, and all other kinds of mayhem. This bird is completely bombproof and a perfect example of my philosophy that birds can get used to anything and people need to stop tiptoeing around them to avoid causing them any stress. Coral Ann has been everywhere and done everything. However, Martha has an extremely busy schedule, and she knows that she could not give Coral Ann the time and attention she needs. So Coral Ann lives with me in a large cage behind the cash register in my store. She is extremely intelligent and loves to manipulate things. She needs many locks on her cage to keep her in there.

In the basement of my store, I have a studio where I do my radio show every week. I have a headset and an ISDN line to communicate with a board operator at the Sirius studio in New York City who takes the live calls from my listeners. I do the show at night after closing my store. While I am doing this, the phones for the store are right in front of me. One night during the show, I noticed that one of the store's phone lines was lit. I wondered how this could be since I was the only person in the store and the doors were locked. I put down my headset, picked up the phone, and heard someone pressing buttons and dialing numbers. I could also hear the normal background sounds of the store. This happened just after a major robbery, and I panicked, thinking there was someone upstairs. I quickly put the headset back on and told my listeners that I would be right back after a commercial break. I rushed upstairs to discover that Coral Ann had gotten out of her cage and was on the counter holding the telephone receiver with one foot and pressing buttons with her beak. I think she was trying to order Domino's pizza, her favorite food. When I got back down to the studio, I did a great show thanks to that little adrenaline rush.

Martha also loves chickens. She has all sorts of breeds, from fancy chickens to egg-laying chickens. When first visiting Martha's home, most people are amazed by the furniture and antiques. I was most impressed by the chicken coop. It was the kind of chicken coop you dream about, a real Martha Stewart chicken coop. The runs were gravel-lined, and the chicken wire was covered with climbing roses. The chickens were in beautiful condition. Most of her chickens were egg layers, and at the end of those runs, she had quite a few extremely ancient chickens—their egg-laying days had obviously ended years ago. Chickens can actually live up to ten years, but even the best laying chicken usually ends up in a soup pot by the time it is two or three. I asked Martha how she ended up with all of those old chickens. She told me those were the retirement coops. When her chickens got too old to lay eggs, they were moved to this retirement home to live out the rest of their lives. She felt that she owed them a comfortable retirement after they had worked so hard laying eggs for her. This goes to show that Martha is a true animal lover and doesn't resort to ending lives when animals are no longer "useful."

Then there are Martha's canaries. She had always owned lots of parakeets but never any canaries. She became interested in canaries about ten years ago, when we did a Christmas special together. The show's theme was the bird scenes from "The Twelve Days of Christmas." I crossed off the seven swans a-swimming and the six geese a-laying as being too involved, and decided to do the partridge in the pear tree, two turtledoves, three French hens, and four calling birds. I had plenty of partridges, but they are ground birds and really can't perch very well. So for that scene we had the partridge sit in Martha's lap. For comic effect, we put a kookaburra in the pear tree; a kookaburra is a large kingfisher from Australia that emits the laughing jungle sounds we are all familiar with from Tarzan movies. The two turtledoves were easy, because these are common house pets. I could not find any French breeds of chicken in time for the show, so I used three Japanese silky chickens, which looked rather French thanks to the pompadours on their heads.

The calling birds were a challenge. In Europe, a calling bird isn't really a breed. It was actually a male finch set out in a little cage to sing and call down wild birds to be trapped. Most calling birds were finches from the genus *Serinus*, usually European goldfinches and European siskins. I thought a common canary would make a good substitute. To make it more festive, I chose four red factored canaries, which I trained to land on a little Christmas wreath. Martha was so entranced by these little canaries that she promptly took them all home.

She built a large aviary for them in her sunroom. They quickly began breeding, and she soon had about fifty canaries. Just like Martha did with her chicken coop, she expanded the aviary into luxurious accommodations. Today, her whole house resonates with the song of canaries. On the left side of her sunroom, the canaries sing and interact in their large aviaries. On the right side, in front of each window, there is a wild bird feeder full of thistle seed with about a hundred American goldfinches (close relatives of the canary). I will never forget the sight of that room filled with flowering plants and canaries on one side and goldfinches on the other. It was a true Martha Stewart moment.

Which are better, horizontal or vertical cages?

As a general rule, birds that do not climb, such as canaries and finches, prefer horizontal cages so that they can fly back and forth. Birds that like to climb, such as psittacines and barbets, will do better in vertical cages. The larger the cage, the better, whether it is horizontal or vertical. Get the biggest cage you can afford that will fit in your house.

What size cage should I buy for my African Grey?

That depends on whom you ask. If you ask some of the people in online bird chat rooms, any cage less than 10 feet long will be too small. My African Grey, Darwin, lives in a cage 20" x 20" x 30" and has happily done so for the past twenty years. Of course, he comes out regularly for free flight exercise, appears on TV, and travels with me, so his life is not limited to that cage. Again, you are the one buying the cage and putting it in your house. As long as it's no smaller than 20" x 20" x 30", he should not feel compromised at all.

Can I house my conure in the same cage with my Amazon?

Anyone who has seen me on TV knows that I have all of my animals mixed up together. This is true at home as well as on TV. I've kept many different combinations of birds together in the same cage, even incongruous species like budgies and rose-breasted cockatoos. In nature, different species of birds mix together. To see this in action, toss some bread crumbs at a park. You will see seagulls, pigeons, sparrows, and starlings darting around, trying to grab crumbs from one another's bills. However, these birds can get away from one another when they want to. Birds are individuals, and some get along better than others. Think of your birds as different individuals rather than different species. If those two individuals can comfortably cohabit in the same cage, by all means try it. The best bird toy is another bird.

If they don't get along, you will know from the get-go. They will need separate cages, but this isn't the end of the world. Some birds are sociopaths, just like some people. You are the best person to make a decision based on the behavior of your particular birds. Don't allow yourself to be influenced by me telling you it's OK to put them together or by some anonymous Internet expert trying to tell you it's not OK—obviously, exercise caution and common sense when introducing *any* animals into a shared environment.

For the past few nights, an owl has been attacking the ducks and chickens in my yard. I've chased it away a few times, but it keeps coming back and has killed several of them. What can I do?

I've been plagued by predators eating my ducks, chickens, pigeons, and cranes since I was a little kid. Unfortunately, there is no way to prevent this aside from keeping your birds in a secure locked enclosure at night. Occasionally, I'd come home late and feel too tired to go out and lock up the birds. They could go into the coop, and as long as the weather was nice, I thought they'd be fine until morning. Invariably, I'd come out in the morning to find one missing or torn to pieces. This is a management issue more than anything else. If your birds are in an open pen, it needs a chicken-wire cover over the top. If the birds are loose during the day, they must be put into an enclosure each night to keep them safe from nocturnal predators.

I want to build a backyard aviary. How do I know which species of birds I can mix together? How much space does each bird need?

Mixing birds together loose in a backyard aviary isn't the easiest situation to manage. Not all birds get along, and some birds that are not supposed to get along actually do. In my backyard aviaries, I've mixed Australian parakeets such as rosellas, red rump parakeets, cockatiels, budgies, white doves, diamond doves, java sparrows, and zebra finches. They live together in the upper part of the aviary. In the lower part I have golden pheasants, button quails, and coturnix quails.

However, if you want to breed birds, a situation like this it won't work because the larger birds will interfere with the nests of the smaller birds. For breeding purposes, you are always better off keeping each pair or species separate.

To estimate how much space each bird needs, pay attention to its behavior. If two or more birds get along tolerably well and have enough room to sit comfortably in a row on a perch without touching one another, then the aviary is large enough. If the birds are pulling feathers out of one another, or some birds seem compromised or have to cling to the wire because they are being bullied, then the aviary is too small or you have too many birds in it. There is no hard and fast rule for this. A pet keeper should know his pets and be aware of whether they are happy in their habitat.

How do you estimate the right size for a bird cage? Is there a general rule?

This is not cut-and-dried. Some birds can get a lot of exercise in a small cage simply by grabbing onto something and flapping their wings hard. Some birds cannot. Male canaries are kept in very small cages when being conditioned for shows. They have two little perches on which to jump back and forth. When sitting on either perch, the bird should be able to stretch one wing in either direction. Its tail should never hit the side of the cage. Again, this is highly interpretive and everyone seems to be an expert. Some people reading these suggestions will be horrified. In their minds, the cage should be far larger than this. This is what I have found to work well in my experience with keeping birds emotionally and

physically happy, in perfect plumage. If you have room for bigger cages and the money to buy them, God bless you. Buy them from me!

My parrot learned how to open the door of his cage and let himself out. Is he a genius bird or do I need a better birdcage?

Birds are extremely curious creatures, and they are always experimenting with the environment. Titmice in Britain learned to open milk bottles left on porches. Seagulls open bags of potato chips, and parrots can open birdcages. If you can open it, the bird can probably open it, too. Your parrot is no more of a genius than the 2-inch English titmouse that opens milk bottles. Get a C-clip from any hardware store and use that to secure the door. Give your bird foraging toys with food hidden inside or puzzle toys so he can satisfy his curiosity about manipulating objects.

Do birds like to sleep on perches or should I give my bird a Happy Hut? Would he like this better?

Some birds, such as parrots and mynahs, nest in cavities. These are best simulated with the Happy Huts sold in pet shops. They provide an advantage over wooden nest boxes because you can keep switching them to wash them out. Years ago, when hill mynahs were very popular pets, it was customary to place a paper bag in the mynah's cage at night. The mynah would crawl inside to sleep.

Some birds become extremely possessive of their cages when provided with a sleeping area like this. They will begin attacking to defend their little roosting site whenever you put your hand in the cage. Obviously, you can remove the roosting site to stop this, but it seems a shame to deprive your bird of his little bedroom. I usually advise placing the Happy Hut inside a separate sleep cage—something smaller than his normal cage. At night, put your bird in the little cage with his Happy Hut, and place the cage in a dark closet. In the morning, the bird will happily come out of his hut because he knows that his big cage and breakfast await him. At night, he will again be happy to go to his little cubbyhole to sleep. In the wild, this is what birds do. You are now the designated driver, taking your bird from his daytime to nighttime habitat. This way, he won't become possessive of his Happy Hut.

Should I put my budgie's cage on the windowsill so that he can watch the birds outside?

There's nothing wrong with that as long as the weather is nice. If there is a strong breeze, he probably won't enjoy it. But if it's a nice day with no wind, it's fine. In a state of nature, birds regularly go to different places and see different things. So, if we give our pet birds more variety, their lives will be more natural. Of course, if it's 20 degrees or 90 degrees, don't leave him on the windowsill. Common sense rules. If there is a draft blowing through the window, ruffling his feathers and blowing his birdseed all over, don't leave him there. It's also a good idea to cover a portion of the cage while it's exposed to the elements so that your bird may retreat if he gets spooked or wants a little shade.

Someone gave me a beautiful antique birdcage. Is it OK to use this for my finches?

Most antique birdcages (technically defined as one hundred years old or more) were originally designed for European finches or other soft-billed birds. Usually constructed from wood, not only are older cages not recommended for psittacine birds such as parrots (that beautiful antique would be reduced to a pile of toothpicks in no time), but they also are likely to contain toxic substances that could harm any bird. Best to repurpose your antique as an elegant planter.

THE CAGED BIRDS SING

Anyone who has visited Chinatown in New York or San Francisco has undoubtedly seen bird enthusiasts carrying tiny bamboo cages housing small soft-billed birds called zosterops or green singing finches. The larger wooden cages are used for larger soft-billed birds, usually Shama thrushes. These cages may look small, but they are designed to maintain the birds in optimum condition. The perches are placed so that the birds can jump back and forth, and the cages can be cleaned and maintained with minimal disturbance to the birds. These birds are placed in these cages to encourage singing. The aviculturists hang them in a garden, and everyone compares the birds' songs to identify the best singer. If these birds weren't 100 percent happy in these cages, they wouldn't sing (although Maya Angelou might disagree).

What kind of perches do you recommend for finches? Someone told me that tree branches were best.

The very best perches for any birdcage are natural tree branches. However, this causes much anxiety for people because they worry that branches are loaded with diseases and pests and must be sterilized before being put in the cage. When I need some perches for my birds, I just go outside and break some branches off the nearest poor tree, trim them to fit the cage, and put them in there, leaves, buds, blossoms, and all. The birds have a grand time chewing and dissecting them. When they are done, I give them new ones. I am not about to engage in any silly debates about the safety of tree branches. The argument is that branches straight off the tree could harbor pathogens, insecticides, and so on, and perhaps they do, but they have never caused a problem for my birds since I was a little boy.

I just rescued a bunch of baby chicks. Can I keep them in a birdcage or do they need something special?

Baby chickens must be kept at a temperature of 95 degrees. It would be very hard to keep them warm enough in a birdcage. The best thing is to make a brooder from a 10- or 20-gallon aquarium, then clip a clamp lamp with a 150-watt bulb to

the side. Place a layer of bedding or pine shavings at the bottom. Feed them baby chick mash and give them a very, very small water dish to ensure that they do not fall in and drown or catch a chill. As a general rule, the babies will need to be under the light for about three weeks. You may ask why they need to be kept at 95 degrees when mother hens walk around a barnyard with their newly hatched chicks trailing after them. But when the babies get cold, the mother will crouch down and the babies will run under her fluffed feathers and stay there until their body temperatures get back to normal. This is called brooding. At that age, they cannot regulate their body temperatures and are dependent on another heat source.

Do you have any tips on how to keep a bird room clean? I feel like I spend half my life vacuuming up seeds and cleaning cages. How do these birds manage to make such a mess every day?

At my house, we keep our birds as contained as possible. The birds are kept in cages designed by a company called King's Cages. These cages have splash guards across the cups and seed catchers at the base and grills at the bottom to prevent the birds from scattering things out of the bottom. We put newspaper in the tray at the bottom, covered by a sprinkle of aspen wood bedding. The aspen catches a lot of the seed shells, feathers, and feather dust. When the birds flap their wings, most of this debris stays at the bottom of the cage instead of flying all over the room. Pine shavings are a little too light and will blow out of the cage. Cat litter is too heavy, and potentially toxic to birds.

You must clean each cage daily. It's not a big job to pull out the trays, roll up the newspaper and shavings, and throw the whole thing in the trash. It also helps to keep a separate vacuum cleaner in the bird room. This way you don't have to get the regular household vacuum cleaner every time you clean. The idea is to be proactive rather than reactive.

If you do a small amount of cleaning every day, you'll stay ahead of the mess. We have lots and lots of birds at our house, but my wife has an efficient system. It takes her only half an hour a day to care for all the birds.

The Importance of Positive Reinforcement

When I was a kid, the few books that were available on bird training were geared toward parakeets (budgies), which were pretty much the only birds we could afford. The primary training method was habituation, the same method that biologists use to get wild mountain gorillas comfortable in their presence. The books advised keeping a new parakeet in a cage in the busiest room of the house until it calmed down enough to eat comfortably in front of people. The next step was to sit for hours with your hand inside the cage. When the bird accepted your hand in the cage, you began offering him food from your hand. Before you knew it, the parakeet would perch on your hand in the cage. You would then allow it out of the cage to fly around the room. The first couple of times, it would bash into walls and furniture and eventually return to the cage. But before you knew it, the bird was flying all over the house, perching on your shoulder, and acting as if it owned the place—which you know was exactly what it thought. For centuries, parrots, macaws, chickens, and ducks were trained this way.

Early falconers probably invented the first bird-training methods. A falconer would catch a wild bird of prey, use leather straps to keep it on his hand, and just sit with the bird until it realized that humans posed no threat. This process is now known as flooding. Once the bird overcame its fear of humans, the falconer switched to positive-reinforcement training. The bird would be taught to respond to a call through the use of food rewards. Today, pet bird training is usually a combination of flooding and habituation. A new bird's wing feathers are trimmed, so it can't fly away and is forced to stay with humans until it overcomes any fear. In time, the bird becomes habituated to humans. The thing that's missing is positive reinforcement. Without this, we have no way to influence the bird's behavior. Ideally, training should include flooding, habituation, and positive reinforcement. This results in a happier bird and a happier pet keeper. The bird will easily understand what behaviors are expected from it.

It's also important to look at the world from the bird's point of view during training. Birds are so different from us. We need to realize that something as simple as petting the bird when he doesn't want to be touched can cause a breakdown in the relationship. Whether it is with another human or another species, communication is always better if we try to see things from the other point of view.

How do I earn my bird's trust? He seems to avoid me no matter what I try.

Have you ever watched people in the park feeding wild pigeons? These pigeons literally climb all over these people, sit on their heads, and take food from their hands. Obviously, these wild birds have learned to trust people who feed them. Habituation is the best way to earn the trust of a pet bird. When I was a child, this was the only bird-training technique known. Methods like wing feather trimming and flooding a bird with human contact were not generally known at that time.

Whether you have zebra finch or an eagle, gain his trust by teaching him to associate your presence with something good, like food. Take the food out of his cage at night. In the morning, when he is good and hungry, place the dish of food in his cage and watch him for half an hour as he eats. If he refuses to eat while you are there, take the food out and try again in the evening. Repeat this exercise. The first step is to get the bird to eat while you are watching. Do this daily. Except for a hummingbird, half an hour of uninterrupted eating is sufficient. If he is too shy to eat while you are right in front of the cage, start by sitting about 6 feet away and  gradually move closer as he comes to accept this arrangement. The key is for the bird to associate you with food, just like the pigeons in the park and the seagulls at the beach associate people with food.

When your bird begins to eat as soon as you put the food in his cage, start putting your hand in the cage and holding the dish while he eats. Do this for half an hour, twice a day. When he is comfortable eating while you hold the dish, then start feeding him from your hand. There is no point in proceeding to the next step in this training until the bird is completely comfortable. If your bird refuses to eat while you watch him, there is no point in trying to coax him to eat while you hold the dish.

The interesting thing about this method is that the bird's response improves exponentially. At first, you will notice a very small improvement, but as your bird starts losing his fear, he will improve much faster. So don't be discouraged at first. You will be pleasantly surprised at the change in your bird's behavior once he learns to associate you with good things in his life. As a child, this amazed me. A bird that was totally panicked when I started training it would happily fly to

my hand as soon as I opened the cage thirty days later. The bird itself decided that you would not hurt it. Animals do not take our word for anything. There is no way you can convince your bird that you mean no harm; only he can make this decision. When that happens, he will be all over you.

What's the best way to train a new baby bird? What is the best age to start?

As a general rule, it is easier to train a younger bird, but tailor your approach to your bird's individual pace. When I was a kid and parakeets were the ubiquitous pet birds, we were always instructed to choose parakeets that still had bars on their foreheads and black tips on their beaks. This meant they were only six weeks old. Parakeets that had lost their stripes and had clear yellow or white foreheads were not "barheads" and were deemed impossible to train. Of course, this wasn't true; they only took longer to train.

Because the barhead parakeets had not yet learned fear of humans, they easily developed a good opinion of them and therefore responded to training more readily. They could more easily mimic human speech because they had not yet mastered all of the normal parakeet sounds.

For the past week, we have had very noisy construction in front of our house and my birds are acting strange and not eating very much. Can this noise be bothering them?

I'm sure it is bothering them, but they will get used to it. They are eating enough to sustain themselves, even if it's less than normal. Realistically, birds can acclimate to just about any variable in their environment. Just look at pigeons and sparrows in busy city streets. Random events are part of life, and it's important that our birds accept this. This way, they won't panic whenever something unusual happens.

Birds are often prey, so their natural reaction is to fly away from anything out of the ordinary. Instinct tells them they will live longer that way. But they can also learn that strange things won't hurt them. If your bird is afraid of the vacuum cleaner, don't move the bird out of the room when you vacuum;

My Mentor, Alba Ballard

I'm often asked how I learned so much about animals with no formal education whatsoever. Much of my information comes from observing animals and keeping all sorts of pets my entire life. But I also learned a great deal from someone I met when I was a teenager. Her family had owned a zoo in Milan, Italy. Even as a child, Alba Ballard could train animals to do just about anything. She showed me pictures of a wolf she had trained to pull her around on a sled and an Andean condor that she led around on a collar and leash, even though the bird was almost three times her size.

She came to the United States, married, had a family, settled on Long Island, and started training birds using the methods she had learned in Europe. She took me under her wing, so to speak, and taught me to observe an animal's behavior and use the information I gathered to either encourage or extinguish the behavior. Alba Ballard lived around the corner from me and had made a name for herself during the 1970s by dressing her birds up as celebrities of the day. Alba's birds were featured on *Late Night with David Letterman* as well as in the Woody Allen movie *Broadway Danny Rose*. Alba's birds even came to my wedding dressed as a bride and groom.

After Alba passed away, she was forgotten by the media and bird people in general, who owe her a debt of gratitude. Much of what she discovered about pet bird husbandry, such as training and diet, is now considered common knowledge. She passed this information on, and many people who practice her bird husbandry methods today really don't know where they originated.

I got a phone call from an author who had stayed with Elizabeth Taylor's daughter and found photos of birds dressed as celebrities. Alba had sent those photos to Elizabeth Taylor thirty years earlier, and this man, Arnie Sven, found them and was fascinated. He tracked me down and called me out of the blue one day. Everyone seems to know me as the bird king. All you have to do is Google *parrots*, and my name will come up four hundred times. I suppose he called me hoping that I would know who had trained those birds in the photos he found.

I told him as much as I could about Alba. He eventually wrote a book called *Mrs. Ballard's Parrots*, which I treasure dearly. I would like to think that Alba is in heaven, content because her teachings have helped me to help so many pet keepers all over the world who see me on TV, listen to me on the radio, or read my books. I miss her dearly and visit her grave every year.

Don't Touch Me

One of the first Amazon parrots I owned as a child was a yellow-fronted Amazon. His name was Papagallo, which means *parrot* in Italian, and this bird was my best friend. I took him everywhere with me. Back then, I didn't know about positive reinforcement or clicker training. He loved me so much that he would fly down from the trees to sit on my head. He did this just because he wanted to be with me. That is real love. However, Papagallo hated having his feathers touched. The most he would tolerate was to sit on my finger and let me rub my nose on his head feathers. But until the day he died, he hated being touched.

Nonetheless, I was constantly trying to touch him. He put up with this endlessly, but finally he would get so aggravated. He would give me a look to say "What part of *don't touch me* can't you understand? You'll understand this!" And—*crunch*—he would give me a good hard bite. After about ten years, Papagallo's negative-reinforcement training finally got through my thick skull.

Because I went through this, I can sympathize with people who own birds that don't like being touched. If this is important to you, get a bird that will enjoy being touched, such as a cockatiel, certain conures, a pigeon, or a duck. All of these birds enjoy being touched. It's a win-win situation.

instead, lean the turned-off vacuum cleaner right up against his cage. After sitting there looking at it in horror for half a day, he will come to realize that it's not going to hurt him, and by the end of the day, he will ignore it totally. More important, the bird won't spend his life afraid of the vacuum cleaner.

I heard that some kinds of parrots are naturally more affectionate than others. Isn't this really a result of how they were raised and socialized?

All parrots have the same kind of brain, and they all look at us in the same way. The problem is that we humans are so vain that we can only relate to animals that express emotions the way we do. We like to hug and touch. Birds have feathers, and animals with feathers don't always enjoy having them touched by dirty, greasy human hands. If a bird doesn't like to be touched, we tend to see this as a lack of affection. In reality, this bird may love you very much, but he just doesn't want you messing up his feathers.

My parrot is so hyperactive, and he's driving me crazy. What can I do to calm this crazy bird down?

In nature, parrots as well as other birds must seek food all day long. When the weather is inclement, they tuck themselves in a tree until it's better. They must then work twice as hard to find a daily supply of food. When kept in captivity, a bird has a lot of pent-up energy that would normally be expended simply trying to survive in its natural habitat. So it's important to find ways to keep the bird busy with toys and foraging mechanisms. Rather than just placing food in his dish, make him work for his food. This is where clicker training can work very well. The bird will learn to perform a particular behavior to earn his food.

If you don't have the time for clicker training, then create some challenges for him. For instance, gift-wrap his food. Take a small piece of apple, wrap it tightly in white paper, and leave it on the bottom of his cage. He will spend a lot of time unwrapping this package before he can eat the apple. This mimics normal foraging behavior. You can use a walnut, a peanut, or a piece of crispy fruit, as soft fruit will soak through the paper. Wrap the piece of food in a piece of plain white paper, and twist the paper tightly around to form a little stem (don't use tape). Parrots and cockatiels will love picking up this package by its little stem, holding it with one foot, and unwrapping it to get the prize inside. As a kid, I hated eating boxes of horrible-tasting Cracker Jack just to get the stupid plastic ring at the bottom, but many birds that normally won't eat a piece of sweet potato or carrot from a dish will eat it if they have to work to get it. If you leave a handful of these prize packages in your bird's cage before you go to work, he will be busy all day.

My bird is only interested in my husband, who oddly wants nothing to do with him. How do I get him to bond with me? I feel like this bird is playing mind games with me.

This is a very common situation, and there is a lot of mythology attached to it. Birds usually prefer the person who spends the most time with them, but not always. When the bird is spending time with his preferred person, just ignore the situation. Your bird will be much more willing to accept you if he

doesn't see you as a rival competing for the attention of its preferred person.

The bird may not love you, but he will come to accept you. When your husband is playing with the bird, stay away. Don't give the bird any reason to think you are interfering in its preferred relationship. If you have ever watched a bird show at a theme park like Busch Gardens, you will see many different handlers working with the birds. I'm sure all of these birds have their favorite trainers, but they willingly work with everyone because everyone respects the birds' wishes. A flock of pair-bonded birds consists of many pairs; however, they all get along and work together. They have their social structure worked out, and they are not worried about other birds stealing their mates.

In the bird's mind, it all boils down to security. If the bird is secure in its relationships, it will be happy. When you husband is not around, that's when you should socialize with the bird.

I got a friend for my parrot to keep him company while I am at work. I thought he would be thrilled, but he seems to hate his new friend. Will they start getting along better if I just leave them together for a while?

The bird doesn't actually have to like the new bird. The mere fact that the birds are in the same room will improve his quality of life. Leave the cages next to each other. Even if the first bird doesn't love the addition, he will still socialize and communicate with another bird. His life will be better with this other bird. With few exceptions, birds are social animals. They may get along better as time goes by. As long as neither one feels threatened or compromised, don't worry about it. I think it is very sad to see a single bird, dog, or gerbil isolated in a house full of humans, with no contact with its own species.

Of course, don't get a second bird unless you have the time and money to care for it. If you do have a single bird, it is not pining away, wishing for a companion. In that animal's mind, it is the last member of its species left on the planet and will live its life as best as it can. Most birds are prey animals and live very close to death. For most birds, if the day goes by without being eaten, it's a good day.

My bird only likes me and will bite anyone else when he gets the chance. How do I get him to be more social?

If the bird only likes you and bites everyone else, it is your responsibility to prevent him from doing this. Whenever he is out of his cage, he should have no opportunity to get near anyone and bite them. If he is in a cage and someone else must feed him, make sure the cage has doors that can be accessed without putting a hand in there. Birds thrive on drama. When your bird is rushing across the floor to attack someone's feet, the resulting drama encourages more of the same from him. Every time this happens, his behavior is reinforced. If he never gets to bite, chase, or frighten people, or cause drama and chaos, in time he will forget that this was ever an option. His reign of terror will end.

My bird screeches like crazy whenever I leave him alone in the room. How do I get him to stop? Can I train him to be quiet on command the way I trained my dog to be quiet?

In a social setting, birds make noise to maintain contact with other members of their species. If your bird is making noise, he does this because he knows you will respond in some way, shape, or form. This may include returning to the room and talking to him, looking at him, or throwing a shoe at his cage to shut him up. The bird doesn't see a flying shoe as something bad. He probably thinks it livens up the day and will make even more noise in the hope that more flying objects will whiz by his cage. Birds only do what works for them. If making noise creates all this drama, your bird will keep it up. As your response becomes more involved, he will make even more noise.

When your bird makes noise, the correct response is to ignore him and walk away. When he is quiet and peaceful, that's when you should shower him with attention. This way he learns that polite, quiet behavior earns the most attention. But this is not a perfect world. There are times when it's impossible to ignore a noisy bird until it quiets down, particularly if it has already learned to associate noise with lots of drama in the house.

No normal bird will make noise if it cannot see. If you have ever attended a Renaissance faire, you have seen falconers carrying hawks or falcons wearing leather hoods to cover their eyes. Because these birds cannot see, they are calm and quiet. With the exception of owls and a few others, birds cannot see in the dark. They don't want to draw attention to themselves if there is a risk of attracting predators. Placing an opaque cover over the cage will quiet the bird down, but if the cover doesn't completely block out the light, the bird will continue making noise. When you cover the cage, don't engage in any drama. Don't even make eye contact. The bird will see this as a reward. Keep the cover folded nearby the cage, and when your bird starts to act up while you are on the phone, calmly cover the cage and finish your conversation. Don't keep the case covered all day!

However, this doesn't teach the bird anything. The bird will not understand that the cage was covered because it was noisy; only positive reinforcement training will accomplish that. The cover will only shut the bird up until you regain your sanity.

Many noisy birds have been surrendered to me by their exasperated owners, who didn't have the time or patience for training techniques. *Never* is a risky word to use, but I've never personally encountered a bird that did not respond to these training methods. There may be an exception to this in my future, but it hasn't happened yet.

Which birds do better if they are kept in pairs? Which ones should not be kept in pairs?

Quite frankly, all birds that we keep as pets normally live in groups in the wild. Realistically, any bird is happier with the company of its own kind, except possibly the canary. The domestication process has altered canary behavior a bit. Unlike with other passerine finches, you never see a male and female canary sitting together, cleaning each other's heads and neck feathers as would a pair of society finches or zebra finches. In the breeding season, a male canary may feed the female, but that's about the extent of their relationship. The fact that they don't behave affectionately doesn't imply that they don't like company. Female canaries do fine in groups. They may pull one another's tail feathers, but they still enjoy gossiping and comparing notes. However, male canaries in breeding condition will fight furiously and should never be kept together. Some people who keep birds in pairs are disappointed if the birds tend to be less focused on their human caretakers, but this situation is much more natural for birds. A singly kept bird may be so utterly lonely that it interacts with humans out of sheer desperation, much like how Tom Hanks's character interacted

with the volleyball Wilson in the movie *Cast Away*. Again, to determine behavioral norms for pet birds, look to wild birds. Pigeons in the park all have mates, but they also happily interact with humans who feed them.

How much do my birds need to sleep each day? Is it the same amount for my cockatiel as my conure?

A bird's need for sleep varies. When the lights go out, the birds go to sleep because they can't do anything else. Here in the northeastern United States, a chickadee may sleep for fifteen hours in December but only five hours in June. Internet debate on this subject is based on anecdotal information. For instance, most parrots come from equatorial regions. It is commonly believed that they must sleep for twelve hours a day because days and nights are twelve hours long at the equator. That may make perfect sense but is not based on scientific study. That said, I really don't keep track of my bird's normal sleeping hours. Regardless of whether we turn the lights out at nine o'clock or twelve o'clock, that's when they go to sleep. When I come home in the afternoon, I sometimes find them taking a bird nap (not a cat nap). I've yet to see my birds suffering from sleep deprivation as a result of the erratic sleep patterns that my busy lifestyle subjects them to.

My bird is suddenly very aggressive around his cage. Did I do something to make this happen?

What you did was threaten his security, and this has made him aggressive. (Although birds can suddenly become aggressive around their cages during the spring months, when their systems are flooded with breeding-cycle hormones. This type of aggression should subside once daylight hours shorten.) If your bird doesn't want you to put your hand in his cage, don't, or you will get bitten. Whether it's a zebra finch or an ostrich, when birds are really angry, they fluff their feathers to appear larger. This behavior stems from the bird's reptilian ancestors that puffed out their throats and crests when alarmed. If your bird is sitting on top of his cage with his tail splayed out, ready to do battle, mist him with a spray bottle. This will cool off his rage and divert his attention. This is not to be used as a punishment, only as a distraction.

However, there will be situations in which you must interact with the bird even if he is possessive of his cage. The best way is to use a simple perch to remove him from his cage. Take him away from the cage and put him on a play stand, and he will usually be fine. Use the same method if you want to get him off the top of his cage. This way, you are interacting with him and he doesn't get an opportunity to bite you. If there is no confrontation, as time goes by, his feelings of possessiveness will subside. Confrontation with anything that bites is unlikely to end on a happy note.

Help! My bird pulls out her feathers. How do I get her to stop?

Reptiles have scales, bats have wings, and turtles have beaks, but only one creature has feathers. And nothing looks more out of place than a bird without feathers. This can be a result of certain physical ailments or self-mutilation. Either way, it causes great worry to bird keepers.

Only birds kept in captivity have the time to go about mutilating their feathers. During their nesting season, certain birds will look for feathers that can be used to line their nests, but they find these on the ground or pull them out of other birds. The only wild birds that pluck their own feathers for this purpose are waterfowl. The eider duck pulls out its own breast feathers to line its nest; these feathers have exceptional insulating properties, and manmade substitutes have never been able to match it.

This behavior is far from rare in captive birds, and I have seen it in every type of bird, from hawks to pigeons to canaries. Some bird experts have stated that it is more common in African Greys, but I don't agree. It may seem more common simply because this species of parrot is more often kept as a pet and more of the behavior is observed in this species as a result.

Feather plucking usually begins when a bird molts and he has access to feathers found on the bottom of his cage. He picks one up and plays with it and finds the process amusing. The next day, he does it again. Eventually, he is finished molting, but he still enjoys playing with feathers, so he starts looking around for more. He takes a look at himself and thinks, *Gee, there are plenty here to play with.* By now, he is in the habit of destroying some feathers every day to keep himself amused. This gives him pleasure, and he has no idea that he looks silly with his feathers plucked out. Plucking the feathers also induces a serotonin rush. As a result, this experimental behavior eventually becomes a full-blown obsession. Once they have managed to pluck out all their feathers, some birds will start pinching themselves to induce this serotonin rush.

Not only does this cause the bird to look awful, but he will be physically compromised as well. Normally, he molts once a year, but as a result of this plucking he will continually be growing new feathers, which takes a toll on his system.

The first step is to take him to a good avian vet for a complete checkup and a blood panel to make sure that the lack of feathers is not due to an underlying physical illness, such as *Giardia* infection. If your bird gets a clean bill of health, the problem is behavioral, and you must pursue modification. Give your bird less time to chew his feathers, and help him find a more satisfying hobby to replace this activity.

1. Limit his time. Cover his cage for ten to twelve hours a day. He will be quiet and sleep, thus cutting in half the amount of time you need to keep him occupied.
2. Mist him with water every day. It takes about three hours for his feathers to dry. He cannot dry his feathers and pluck them at the same time, and it's no fun playing with soggy feathers. So, if you mist him twice a day, he is prevented from indulging in any feather plucking for six hours. Some birds, such as cockatoos, have a lot of powder in their feathers and don't wet easily. Add a few drops of bird shampoo to the mister as a wetting agent.
3. Help him find another outlet. Many birds enjoy clicker training and look forward to learning in this manner. This is also one good way to break up his day. Of course, it doesn't work for all birds. Ray Berwick's cockatoo La La starred in the *Beretta* TV series. Even though that bird was busy working every day, he still found time to chew his wings and tail feathers. Dr. Irene Pepperberg's African Grey Alex also chewed his feathers despite a busy schedule. Dr. Pepperberg is a brilliant scientist who wrote the book *Alex and Me*. She trained Alex to talk, which in itself is no great accomplishment. However, she did prove to the scientific community that birds have cognitive reasoning ability. The Austrian animal behaviorist Konrad Lorenz had written about this extensively in the 1930s and 1940s, but apparently everybody forgot about that. Through her research, Dr. Pepperberg confirmed the theories that Konrad Lorenz had first described decades earlier.

If training doesn't interest your bird, try to interest him in different toys. Get a lot of different toys and rotate them so that he always has different ones. These don't need to be fancy, expensive bird toys. A box of popsicle sticks or toothpicks makes a great bird toy. Dump them in the bottom of the cage, and the bird will spend hours picking them up and chewing them. Many birds love

Clicker Training

The first step in clicker training a bird to perform a specific behavior is to teach it to associate the click with a food reward. It's easier to do this when the bird is hungry. Use a treat that it can eat very quickly. You don't want it sitting there pecking away at something for ten minutes. Put the bird on a perch, stand in front of it, give it a treat, and click. Keep repeating this until the bird associates the sound with a forthcoming treat. Now let's assume that we want to teach our bird to pick up a miniature American flag, hold it in his beak, and walk with it. You can only clicker train an animal to do a behavior that is natural for it. But you have no way of explaining this to the animal. You must patiently wait for the animal to perform that behavior, which you then reward.

Have a handful of treats in one hand and the clicker in the other. Put the bird on a table and set the flag on the table next to it. Just sit there and wait until the bird becomes curious and reaches out to touch the flag. As soon as the bird shows interest or tries to pick it up, click and give it a treat. Soon, the bird will expect a treat whenever it touches the flag. The next step is to shape the behavior by giving the rewards more selectively. Instead of rewarding the bird when it touches the flag, only click and reward when it tries to pick it up in his beak. It is a step-by-step process to gradually shape the behavior by rewarding actions that the bird does naturally. Eventually, the bird will only get a treat when he picks up the flag and walks with it in his beak.

to pick the threads out of little squares of cloth. Cut a piece of fabric up very small so that there are no threads that could tangle around his legs. Put them in a cup and let him pick them apart.

Another way to prevent feather plucking is to fit the bird with a plastic collar, similar to the Elizabethan collars that are put on dogs after surgery. This may be the best choice if the bird is seriously mutilating himself to the point that he is bleeding. Unfortunately, it will need to be left on the bird for about a year until his wounds completely heal and his feathers grow back. Removal of the collar must be done gradually; take off the collar for short periods every day and provide diversions. Otherwise, the bird will go right back to feather plucking when he has the opportunity.

A new option that has also proven effective is a homeopathic remedy called Pluck No More. When I first heard of this, I was highly skeptical. I couldn't understand how the bird could ingest something that would change an established behavior pattern. However, this is not snake oil or expensive water. There are active ingredients, and it has actually been banned for sale in Japan, because the homeopathic ingredients in Pluck No More are considered prescription substances there. They are not available over the counter like homeopathic remedies in this country. I mention this because Pluck No More is sometimes derided as nothing more than expensive water. If that were the case, it would be perfectly legal in Japan.

I spoke to the scientist who developed Pluck No More. He explained that it does not enter the bird's bloodstream. Instead, it acts on the nervous system at the base of the tongue and throat to replicate the serotonin rush produced by feather plucking. I have seen it work, and I am no longer a skeptic. While it does not work for every bird, it may be an option available to you.

You need to experiment. Feather plucking is a highly individualized situation. Every bird is different, and advice on this subject ranges from realistic and useful to ridiculous and ineffective. The fact is that some pet birds will always pluck their feathers to some extent. If it isn't compromising the bird's health, sometimes you just have to live with it. The bird doesn't care if his feathers are a mess. A pet bird doesn't need his feathers to fly or keep warm outdoors or compete in a bird show. More likely, your friends and relatives will have

something to say about it. But every family has a few dysfunctional members. We may roll our eyes, but we accept them as they are.

My African Grey seems to be some kind of trained attack parrot. He is so sweet and affectionate with me, but he goes ballistic when he sees a stranger. Are they all like this?

Not all African Greys act this way; mine doesn't. Dr. Irene Pepperberg's African Greys don't act like that, and neither do all of the African Greys in bird shows. Of course, these birds are treated like birds, not little feathered people. This is the biggest mistake that most pet keepers make. If your African Grey behaves aggressively toward strangers, it's because he's learned that this behavior elicits the response he seeks. If he lashes out and grabs the bars when a stranger approaches his cage, and the stranger quickly backs away, the bird soon discovers that this is a fun thing to do. The bird is in control of the situation.

It's important not to respond to the bird's territorial behavior. If your guests want to interact with the bird, they should pick him up with a stick rather than offering him a hand. Biting the stick will not elicit the response that the bird is looking for. Animals don't waste their energy on useless endeavors. But many people seem to enjoy the antics of an aggressive bird. They encourage this behavior and brag about how their bird likes only one person and goes out of its way to hurt other people. I have seen many online videos of parrots chasing people across a room. Obviously, someone is getting a kick out of this. It's not up to me to judge these people. If that's what turns them on, God bless them. But I personally want all my pets to be calm and friendly. You never know when someone else may need to care for them. And I think birds are much happier if they perceive all humans as friends.

My cockatoo bites me really hard when I play with him. Is there a way to make him stop?

It's hard to say, without seeing exactly what is happening. Some birds are extremely orally fixated and love to chew toys and manipulate things. They will go for your fingernails and rings. I've seen people curl their fingers and turn the stones around on their rings when handling these birds. This only encourages the bird to try harder. Anyone who observes birds interacting will occasionally see bird A nip the toe or pull the crest feathers of bird B. Bird B screams and conks bird A on the head, and it stops. I am not recommending that you conk your bird on the head. But if he keeps playing roughly, tell him no or blow in his face and redirect him to a toy (but do not lean your face close to the bird, for obvious reasons). If your bird is in a mouthy mood when you interact with him, redirect him to a jingly toy, plastic baby keys, or a Dixie cup. If he doesn't get any opportunities to bite your fingers, rings, or watch during play, he will stop seeing this as an option.

Bird Doctors

Although birds have been kept as pets for centuries, veterinary care for them is a recent innovation. Only in the past twenty years have we developed a good understanding of bird diseases and medical issues. Before then, medical care for birds consisted mostly of trial and error. When I look at older bird-care books from the 1950s and 1960s, it's interesting to see some of the things that were labeled as diseases, such as sour crop. It was assumed that the food given to the bird was bad and could not be digested, causing the crop to become sour. In reality, the bird could not digest the food in its crop because of a bacterial infection. This wasn't understood until it became common to do cultures to identify bacteria in the bird's system in order to find the proper antibiotic treatment.

Birds are also very good at masking their illnesses. An ailment may not become noticeable until the bird is actually dying. This is unfortunate for the bird, the owner, and the veterinarian. Very often, avian veterinarians don't get the opportunity to treat a bird until it is dying, and that definitely limits his options. He then gets blamed for killing the bird, when the owner should have taken it to the vet much sooner. Avian veterinarians have a much harder job than vets who specialize in mammals do. It's much harder to look like a hero when most of your patients are brought to you on the brink of death. But we are trying to change misconceptions about bird health care to ensure that our pet birds live longer, healthier lives.

If you brought your bird to the vet every year for a culture and blood test, the vet would have a baseline to evaluate the bird's current state of health. It would be much easier to know if something was cooking inside the bird that was likely to compromise its health. Many problems could be nipped in the bud.

Surgical procedures for birds have also advanced considerably in recent decades. Back in the 1970s, the normal bird anesthesia was an injection of ketamine, a hallucinogenic drug. The bird passed out, the vet did the surgery as quickly as possible, and everyone hoped the bird would wake up. Today, anesthetic protocols for birds are quite precise. Surgical instruments are also much more precise and delicate. Ultramagnification permits fine surgical procedures and suturing. Of course, we still don't know everything about sick birds. But we know a lot more than we did several decades ago. And I am sure we'll know even more a few decades from now, thanks to talented, dedicated avian veterinarians.

How do I find an avian veterinarian?

This is hard because many vets are not avian vets specifically. A real avian vet must have extensive hands-on experience with birds. He must be part magician, fortune-teller, and gambler. The best way to find a good avian vet in your area is to check the Association of Avian Veterinarians' Web site: www. aav.org. Another great resource might be a local pet store that has a lot of birds. The trouble with asking only individuals with pet birds is that many of them wait until a bird is dying before actually taking it to a vet. Of course, if the poor bird dies, that vet is often blacklisted. That's not a fair test for any vet. You need to ask someone who has a lot of birds and who constantly goes to the vet for care and advice. Whomever you choose, don't ignore your gut reaction; if the individual does not seem knowledgeable or compassionate, keep looking.

What kind of first aid can I give my bird if I notice that he is sick or injured?

Unfortunately, there really isn't anything you can do at home; he must be seen by a professional. If a bird isn't feeling well, he will fluff out his feathers because his body temperature has fallen. His energy reserves must be used to maintain his body temperature and stay warm rather than to fight the infection. So, when you notice that your bird is unwell, put him into a hospital cage. Put a 150-watt lightbulb in a clamp lamp and affix it to the side of the bird's cage. Cover the top and three sides with a blanket to raise the air temperature in the cage to 95 degrees. Now the bird can use his energy to fight the infection until you can get him to the vet. You have essentially stopped the bird from dying. Birds that have suffered trauma, such as breaking a wing or leg crashing into a window, or injuries from a dog or cat, will also benefit from this. The bird's body temperature can drop from shock.

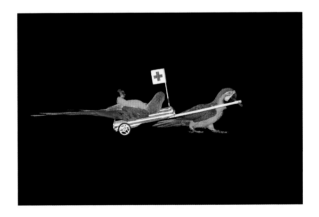

Your bird's medicine chest should contain a clamp lamp and a working 150-watt bulb. It's very disconcerting to discover that you have no working lightbulbs in the house when you are trying to make a hospital cage at ten o'clock at night.

You should also have a bottle of coagulant powder like Kwik Stop. If your bird breaks a talon or the tip of his beak, this will stop the bleeding immediately.

Hydrogen peroxide should also be on hand to wash wounds. Avoid using antibiotic creams and salves. These will get all over the bird's feathers and compromise his ability to stay warm.

I just got a new bird, and I was told not to put him in with my other birds for two weeks. Is this necessary? He looks fine, and I hate to leave him all by himself.

Back in 1970s, I ran many quarantine stations for the federal government. At these stations, the animals are in pure quarantine. Once they go in, nothing comes out, not even trash. We had to shower before going in and again before coming out. The birds remained in these stations for thirty days, sometimes longer if the test results were delayed. These safety measures prevented the potential spread of any airborne pathogen that the birds may have brought into the country. At the time, the biggest concern was Newcastle's disease, a chicken disease.

I cannot imagine how keeping a bird in a separate room of the house would be an effective quarantine measure. If your bird harbors any virus or bacteria that can be transmitted by air, that pathogen is in your home as soon as the bird enters. There is only one way to ensure that a new bird is not carrying any transmissible pathogens. Purchase the bird and take him to an avian vet for swabs and a blood test. Then take him back to the pet shop or leave him at the veterinary clinic. When those test results are back, and the vet gives him a clean bill of health, then you can take him home without fear of spreading disease to your other birds.

This is an extreme measure, to be sure; you can also use common sense. Look at the other birds in the pet store before you make a purchase. Are they clean and healthy? Does the bird you want look OK? If he doesn't look healthy, you wouldn't buy him, right? However, remember that birds can and do mask diseases very well. If you really want peace of mind that your new bird is pathogen free, only an avian vet can guarantee this.

I was told that my bird's beak and claws need trimming. How do I do this?

In nature, a bird's beak and claws never need trimming because they are constantly worn down through use. In captivity, all birds from eagles to penguins need some manicuring from time to time. The avicultural word for this is *coping*, an old falconry term. You cope a bird's beak or nails. One of my few dubious talents is the ability to cope the beaks and nails of just about any bird on the planet with one hand. This talent never really got me anywhere, but it will be a nice thing to put on my headstone.

But even I can make mistakes when coping a bird's bill. A pet bird owner can safely trim a bird's nails; if you cut one a bit short and it bleeds, you can put some Kwik Stop powder on it. But if you make a mistake and accidentally cut the bird's tongue, it can easily bleed to death. Beak trimming should always be done by an expert.

How often should I trim my bird's nails or wing feathers?

This depends on the individual bird. Some birds have very fast-growing beaks and nails. For instance, my African Grey, Darwin, needs his nails trimmed every six weeks despite the fact that he has plenty of rough tree branches and perches in his cage. On the other hand, Remus, my hyacinth macaw, has never needed trimming in the thirty years I've owned him.

Some bird owners don't trim their bird's nails often enough. The nails will grow around in a circle, like a ram's horn, which can be very dangerous.

These nails can get caught on the cage bars, causing the bird to break a leg. Then there are owners who trim their bird's nails too often. They don't like the feel of the bird's sharp nails and keep them way too short. People bring birds into my store, insisting that they need nail trimming when they really don't. In that case, I smooth the nails with an emery board rather than make them shorter. If the nails are too short, the bird can't even grasp its perch and will keep slipping off. Only once I have approved of keeping a bird's nails short and flat. One of my customers was taking blood-thinning medication, which makes the skin very thin and soft. In that instance, there was a valid reason for this extreme bird grooming.

The schedule for wing feather trimming depends on your bird's molting cycle. The molting process takes about three months to complete. Wild birds molt at predictable seasonal times, after breeding and before migration. For pet birds born indoors, this cycle is harder to predict. They will molt one year after they are born. It is important to keep track of when your bird molts in order to know when to trim his wing feathers. For instance, if his normal molting period is from April to June, and you trim his wing feathers in April, they will grow right back along with the rest of his feathers. But if you wait until July, the wing feathers won't need trimming again for a year. This is one good reason to pay attention to when your bird molts. Save the feathers to make sure he has molted properly and to ensure that there are no feathers lying on the bottom of his cage as a temptation to chew.

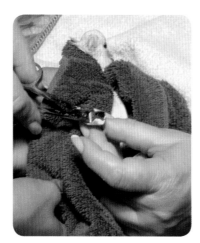

The last time I trimmed my bird's nails, one started to bleed. I couldn't hold him still long enough to apply the styptic powder to his bleeding nail. What is the best way to do this?

Get a cardboard box that is just large enough for the bird to comfortably stand inside. Line the bottom with a flat layer of paper towels and sprinkle the powder all over the paper towel. Put the bird in the box, and close the lid. Since the bird is in total darkness, he will

Blood Feathers

When a bird molts, each feather falls out of its feather follicle and a new one starts to grow, similar to the way in which a deer grows a new set of antlers. These new feathers are nourished by blood vessels. When a feather reaches its full length, the blood vessels in the quill recede into the body and seal off. If the feather breaks during its growth cycle, the blood will ooze from the break. Notice that I say ooze, not gush. People panic when they see a broken blood feather because they don't understand what it is. A bird will not usually bleed to death from a broken blood feather. It will eventually clot on its own if you leave the bird alone. But people panic and try to discover where the blood is coming from. If the bird breaks a blood feather in its wing and folds the wing, the blood will ooze onto the bird's side, making it look like the side rather than the wing is actually bleeding.

In nature, this happens all the time. And birds do not plummet from the sky when they break a blood feather. Eventually, the feather breaks off and the bird has a broken feather stub until it molts. If your pet bird breaks a blood feather, cover the cage and leave the bird in darkness for a short while; the bird will be still and the bleeding should soon stop. (However, if you notice continued bleeding, take your bird to the vet, as significant blood loss could lead to problems.) It's not unusual for a bird to flap around its cage if something startles it during the night. In the process, it breaks a blood feather, and in the morning, you find blood on the cage, the walls, and the ceiling. Don't panic; this looks worse than it is. Cover the bird's cage until the bleeding stops. Have an avian vet or a professional groomer remove the feather stub.

When everything is under control and you start cleaning up the mess, use hydrogen peroxide to clean the blood off of the cage, perches, and bird toys. Wipe everything down with hydrogen peroxide, and the blood spots will bubble and sizzle and come right off. If your bird has blood on his feathers, wipe them with a wet paper towel soaked in hydrogen peroxide. And here's a handy laundry hint from the pet keeper: if there are blood stains on your clothes, put some hydrogen peroxide on the stains and let them sit for a few minutes. Later, when you put them in wash, they will come out nice and clean.

stand still, with his bleeding toe in constant contact with the powder. Even if he walks around, it will still adhere to his bleeding nail. The box must be just large enough for the bird to stand. If the box is too big, the bird will flap his wings and the styptic powder may fly into his eyes, causing irritation. When used correctly, this trick works for any bird with a short nail. However, if you do accidentally trim your bird's nail too short, don't feel like you did anything wrong. It happens to me all the time.

My canary was a beautiful color until he molted. Now his feathers are all weird and patchy and they don't match. Is he going to stay like this?

The color of some canaries is artificially enhanced with a food coloring that will change yellow canaries orange, and orange canaries red. The next time the bird molts, these artificially enhanced feathers will fall out and the new feathers will be the natural color. Even if the color of the bird's feathers changes, feather quality should remain the same regardless of whether he is eating the colored food. In rare cases, a canary's feathers can be compromised due to an iodine deficiency or other physical problem. This can only be determined through an examination by an avian vet.

My bird fell on the floor, and I noticed he has a wound under his tail. Does this need to be stitched by a vet?

This is known as broken tail syndrome. This happens when a bird's wing feathers are clipped a little too short and the bird subsequently falls on a hard tile or wood floor. This causes the wing to hit against the skin right below the tail, causing a cut.

Because wing feather trimming has affected the bird's balance, he keeps falling. Every time he jumps out of his cage or off your shoulder and hits this hard floor, he reinjures that spot and the cut gets a little bigger. If the cut gets large enough, yes, it will need to be stitched. If the injury is fresh and new, it may heal on its own. You have to make sure that the bird has no more falls for at least four weeks. This is not easy to do, and it may be better to keep the bird in his cage for that four-week period to ensure that he is totally healed. If you want to take the bird out, put the cage on a carpeted surface so there is no chance he will fall.

Someone offered me a good deal on a parrot with a few missing feathers. I was told he would be fine when he molts. Should I go for the deal?

When a bird is molting, it rarely looks as though his feathers are compromised. In the wild, the only birds that looks compromised when molting are waterfowl like ducks and geese. They lose all of their wing feathers at one time when they molt in the summer. Some birds, such as Amazon parrots, will look a little scruffy when molting, but the scruffiness includes the entire bird, even the head feathers. If a bird has scruffy body feathers and perfect head feathers, that bird is mutilating his feathers rather than molting. A bird that is mutilating his feathers will still have perfect head feathers because he can't reach them. I have seen a few cockatoos pull out their crest feathers with their feet, but this is the exception, not the rule.

I've had my Cockatoo for thirty years, and recently the skin on his feet has started looking as aged as my own. Do you think a little baby oil would take care of this dryness and scaliness?

You should *never* apply any oil to your bird. Birds have glands that excrete small amounts of natural oil, which they rub through their feathers one by one. Many birds also have powder downs under their feathers that release a fine powder when they break off. This powder conditions the bird's legs and feet and also gets all over the glass and stainless steel surfaces in your home.

Any oil or greasy substance applied to the bird's feet or legs will inevitably get all over his feathers and compromise his ability to retain body heat. This is how seabirds are killed by oil spills. They swim through the oil slick, it gets in their feathers, and they freeze to death because the feathers clump together and no longer keep them warm.

However, some older birds tend to develop dry, scaly legs. The only substance that can be safely applied to your bird's beak or feet is natural beeswax. Put a bit on your fingertips and gently rub it onto his beak and legs. This is what pigeon breeders apply to the beaks and legs of their birds before a show to make them look so polished and shiny.

Is it better for my bird to have a bath or a shower? How often is good? Does this prevent him from getting bird mites?

Bird mites and feather mites are actually very rare. If your bird does have them, a bath or shower will only ensure that the mites are very clean. Only insecticides like Sevin or Pyrethrin will eradicate these external parasites.

All of my birds are bathed daily whether they like it or not. Some birds don't like it, but you need to ensure that your bird bathes every day to maintain its feathers in good condition. Most passerine birds such as finches and canaries prefer to bathe in a dish of still water. Be sure to remove this water as soon as your bird finishes because you don't want him drinking it. Some parrots prefer to bathe in a very small dish, such as a drinking dish on the side of the cage. They seem to be afraid of large volumes of water. Possibly in their native jungle habitat, they were more likely to be eaten by an alligator if they bathed in a large body of water. Some birds like to bathe in the sink;

others prefer to be misted with warm water. Tap water may contain iron or high contents of other minerals, so pure bottled water is probably best for misting your bird. When misting a bird, never spray him directly. Use very warm water and spray it up so it falls on the bird like a gentle rain.

Some birds, such as African Greys, cockatoos, and cockatiels, have a great deal of powder in their feathers, which repels water like the oil in a duck's feathers, making it harder to wet these birds. You can find feather shampoos at most pet shops. These act as a wetting agent: put a few drops in the spray bottle with the water, and the bird will be thoroughly wetted when you mist him. Because the ingredients are very pure and mild, there is no need to rinse. It will be distributed evenly through the bird's feathers as he grooms them.

How do I get my bird to take a bath? I got a birdbath for my budgie, but he won't go near it. I thought all birds loved taking baths.

Budgies are native to the Australian desert. The little water that is available usually has some kind of predator lurking nearby. Most budgies roll around in wet leaves in the rain to bathe. Many times, I put a big wet lettuce leaf in with my budgies, and they love to jump on it and roll around. Realistically, I don't always have time for that, so I will mist them with a plant sprayer.

If the bird starts rolling on the wet lettuce leaf as soon as you put it in the cage, that's fine. But that doesn't always happen. The bird may not be in the mood for a bath, and you can't leave the leaf in there for too long. You don't want the bird trying to eat dirty wilted lettuce that is lying in the bottom of his cage. It's a matter of hygiene. I enjoy watching my birds roll on the leaves and fluff out their feathers, but if they don't want to do that, I would rather not leave wet lettuce in the cage. If my birds want some greens, I would rather give them something nutritious like watercress, chicory, or dandelion greens. Dark, bitter, leafy greens are much healthier for them.

Do all birds have lice and mites? What's the difference? Can my other pets catch these from my birds?

Most animals have parasites peculiar to their species. If by chance your bird did have feather lice or scaly face mites, your dog or cat is not going to catch either.

Feather lice are insects that actually eat the bird's feathers. Mites are arachnids like spiders. They suck the bird's blood. These parasites are quite uncommon in cage birds, aside from the scaly face or scaly leg mite, which burrow under the skin on the bird's legs and around the bill. A parakeet or canary with scaly legs or growths on its bill usually has a mite infestation. In the past, this was extremely difficult to cure. We used to apply toxic, foul-smelling oils to the bird, hoping to smother the mites. But this didn't always work because of the layer of hardened skin between the oil and the mites. Now there is a wonderful drug called Ivermectin, available from your vet, to treat scaly leg or scaly face mites. Sometimes one dose will magically clear up the problem. If you do notice that your bird has a scaly face or scaly legs, take him to the vet right away—although it is easily treated, it is also extremely painful.

Can I catch any diseases from my bird? What about bird flu?

Bird flu comes in two forms. The high-pathogen form, the one we read about in the papers, has caused a horrific economic crisis throughout the world. The low-pathogen form of bird flu is found in just about every live poultry market in the world. This type cannot be transmitted from birds to humans.

In a few cases, the high-pathogen form of bird flu has been transmitted from birds to humans, mainly in Southeast Asia. The number of cases is incredibly small. However, the panic it causes has led well-meaning but ineffective governments to implement policies that cause economic hardship by restricting the movement of birds from one country to another. This is more a result of media sensationalism than any actual health risk.

There are a few other ailments, like psittacosis and pigeon keeper's lung, that can be transferred from birds to humans, but these are rare. If they posed a real health hazard, it would be illegal to sell or keep birds as pets. People have kept pet birds for thousands of years, and at this point it seems pretty unlikely that birds will wipe out the human race. But Alfred Hitchcock may disagree with me.

What is parrot fever?

Parrot fever is the layman's term for psittacosis, which is also known as ornithosis or bird chlamydia. This is one of the potentially fatal diseases in birds that can also be transmitted to humans. It is easily treatable with chlortetracycline. It does pop up in human populations occasionally, inevitably causing a flurry of sensational media stories, but it is rare. I've had birds from other countries, caught and banded wild birds for the federal government, kept every kind of pet bird, and slept among birds, and in my entire life I have yet to contract parrot fever. Either I am immune, or it really is just as rare as I say it is.

Feathered Friends

The technical term for bird keeping is *aviculture*, which in-cludes keeping and breeding birds in a captive situation. Birds have been kept in cages for hundreds of years, but this is not pet keeping in my opinion. When birds are kept in cages, this precludes social interaction between humans and pets, and that interaction is what pet keeping is all about. A canary breeder may love his birds, but not as individuals. He may appreciate a particular bird's type and quality, but he doesn't give that bird a name. It is known by the number on its leg band. This is aviculture.

Throughout my life, all of my birds have had names and they have all had individual relationships with me. This seems odd to some people because they don't credit birds with much intelligence. But even chickens on a farm understand when humans are coming to feed them or grab one for the soup pot. If you watch a flock of pigeons, crows, or seagulls, you see that the birds know each other as individuals. The same applies to birds kept in a human family. A pet bird recognizes the family members and the other pets in the home. I've seen pet birds amuse themselves by calling dogs over to their cages and tossing seed on the floor for the dogs to eat. Birds such as canaries and finches may not seem as interested in social interaction with humans, but they still respond when you put fresh greens in the cage. This interaction breaks up the monotony of their day and gives them something to look forward to.

Depriving your bird of social stimulation leads to feather plucking or other obsessive-compulsive disorders. This is why it is so important to interact and do fun things with your bird. This can be something as simple as whistling or talking to him as you feed him. Of course, there are also people who take interaction to the other extreme and shower with their parrots.

You should spend some fun time with your bird each day, but switch it up from time to time. In nature, a bird's situation varies every day. Some days it rains and there is no food, some days it's too windy to fly, and some days it's warm and sunny. For pet birds, social interaction with humans should also vary. This way, the bird accepts it as a random event and doesn't feel entitled to it. If for some reason the bird is then deprived of your attention for a few days, he will be able to accept it rather than resort to obsessive behavior.

Which birds are the easiest to teach to talk? Which are the hardest?

No bird can be taught to talk in the same way that people talk. However, some have a talent for mimicking sounds. No one seems to know why. For instance, among the passerine birds, starlings, mynahs, and mockingbirds can all mimic. The name *mockingbird* comes from its habit of mocking the songs of other birds. But why can a mynah bird say actual words, while a starling can imitate whistles and other bird songs but does a poor imitation of human words, and the mockingbird mimics whistles and bird calls but cannot imitate human words at all? Why can a yellow-naped Amazon talk, sing, and say so many words but an orange-wing Amazon at best can say six or seven? Why can a male cockatiel talk but not a female? Female yellow-naped Amazons can talk as well as the males can, so why can't a female cockatiel whistle? Well, it's because certain parrots have an innate courtship song. When male parakeets (budgies) and cockatiels are separated from their peers at an early age, their courtship song incorporates sounds they learn from their human peers. Female cockatiels and parakeets have no courtship song and cannot imitate human words at all. So the mimicry of a cockatiel or parakeet is different from the mimicry of a yellow-naped Amazon, blue-and-gold macaw, or hill mynah. In those species, both sexes can mimic equally well.

People have kept birds for thousands of years and have discovered that certain species such as African Grey parrots; the yellow-naped, double yellow-headed, and blue-fronted Amazons; and mynahs are better at mimicking human speech. If a bird is going to talk, this will happen whether or not you teach it. Naturally, if a bird has a talent for mimicry, he will learn much more. When I was young, I had an African Grey named Coco, who I taught to recite the entire Jack and Jill nursery rhyme. But I had plenty of time in those days. My current African Grey, Darwin, says many words, but I haven't taught him any. He simply repeats what he hears the most, and that can be dangerous in mixed company!

My bird whistles, but I'd like to teach him to talk. How long does it take for a bird to talk?

Some birds, such as a red-lored Amazon, can only whistle. Others, such as the yellow-naped Amazon and the African Grey, can whistle and imitate words very well. It's a lot easier for a bird to whistle than emulate human speech. If you make a big fuss over the bird whenever he whistles, he will continue to do this. Why should he do the harder work if the easy work earns him plenty of attention? If you don't want your bird to whistle, don't encourage it. When he starts whistling, walk away from him. When he starts making any other sounds that seem like he is trying to mimic words, give him attention and praise. Keep repeating the word you want him to say. Pets do the things that get them what they want, like food or attention. And they will always do the easiest thing to earn this reward. If you reward the easy behavior, he isn't motivated to try anything more difficult.

Is it true that my bird won't ever learn to talk if he has other birds around?

Every spring, I raise baby Amazon parrots. They are kept in groups of twenty or more, and I never go out of my way to teach them to talk. But as they are growing up, some will start imitating human words. I cannot say why some birds do this naturally and others don't. Bird mimicry has never been completely understood. The only scientist to formally study bird

WORDS IN THE WILD

In the wild, mockingbirds and Australian lyre birds will imitate the sounds of other birds, but there are no documented cases of wild parrots making sounds outside of their normal repertoire. Quaker parrots kept as pets will say many words, but the wild Quaker parrots in Brooklyn hear just as much human speech—yet you will never hear a wild Brooklyn Quaker parrot making sounds other than normal parrot chatter. However, in a situation where the parrot regards humans as friends and protectors, the situation can change.

FLATBUSH AVE.

mimicry was Dr. Irene Pepperberg with her African Grey Alex. Even the great Austrian scientist and animal behaviorist Konrad Lorenz didn't devote time to studying it. For now, our information on bird mimicry of human speech is entirely anecdotal rather than scientific.

If a pet bird is going to talk, it's going to do this whether you teach it to or not, and regardless of whether it's kept alone or with other birds.

Can birds teach one another to talk?

A bird can hear words said by another bird and learn to repeat them. However, this is never done intentionally. If a bird is inclined to mimic, it will imitate whatever sounds it is regularly exposed to. Some birds imitate doorbells, barking dogs, beepers, cell phones, and microwave ovens. To the bird, these are merely sounds. They can associate particular sounds with objects and events in the 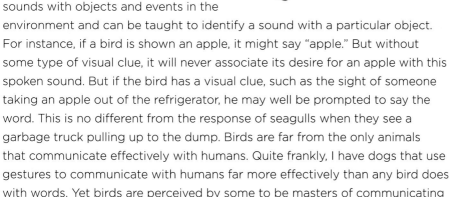 environment and can be taught to identify a sound with a particular object. For instance, if a bird is shown an apple, it might say "apple." But without some type of visual clue, it will never associate its desire for an apple with this spoken sound. But if the bird has a visual clue, such as the sight of someone taking an apple out of the refrigerator, he may well be prompted to say the word. This is no different from the response of seagulls when they see a garbage truck pulling up to the dump. Birds are far from the only animals that communicate effectively with humans. Quite frankly, I have dogs that use gestures to communicate with humans far more effectively than any bird does with words. Yet birds are perceived by some to be masters of communicating with humans.

I inherited a lovely parrot from my grandfather. He is very nice, but I am mortified by his vocabulary. Will he eventually stop saying some of these things?

Any bird will imitate swear words because of the drama that ensues among humans when he makes these particular sounds. To a bird, a word is just another sound. If the bird succeeds in creating drama and getting attention with a sound, he will continue to prefer making that sound. This is also why birds enjoy making very loud bird noises: the louder the noise, the more drama it elicits from humans. And this translates into more fun for the bird. If your bird imitates a swear word, your best response is to turn your back and ignore him. Why should he keep repeating that noise if your only response is silence? When he says something that you consider more acceptable, such as "pretty bird" or "I love you," you should respond with praise and attention. In time, he will learn which sounds evoke the most attention and admiration from you.

At the pet shop, I saw a lovebird that seemed to talk pretty well. But I can't seem to teach mine to say a word. What am I doing wrong?

I personally have owned thousands of lovebirds. Out of all of those birds, only one, a peach-faced lovebird, could mimic anything close to a human sound. And all he could do was wolf whistle. So I really cannot comment on this because I have never been able to teach a lovebird to talk.

The lovebird that you saw in the pet shop was obviously unique if it was

mimicking human speech. However, many small birds such as lovebirds, cockatiels, and parakeets have elaborate, interactive chattering songs. Many people misinterpret these sounds as human words. A creature that is three inches long and weighs two ounces, such as a lovebird, would have great difficulty imitating human speech in a tone deep enough to be understood by humans. This however, is very easy for a 2-pound yellow-naped Amazon or a blue-and-gold macaw.

The quality of a bird's voice is usually dependent on the size and weight of the bird. Many children have brought their parakeets into my store, bragging about how many words it can say. When I listen to these birds, I only hear them muttering chattering the usual parakeet chitchat. Yet these children definitely discern human words in this melody of chitchat and bird sounds. Of course, I always agree and praise them for teaching their bird to say three hundred words. I will do whatever it takes to redirect a child's interest from the Internet to the natural world, even if it means telling a little white lie.

Every time I let my bird out to fly around the house, I lose him. Is there any way to keep track of him?

You are losing your bird because you don't keep your eyes on him when he is out. Birds, like puppies, should not be left unsupervised in the house when loose. Don't let the bird out of his cage unless you have the time to watch him. Always catch him before you answer the phone or turn your back on him for any reason. It is your responsibly as a pet keeper to provide a safe flying environment for your bird. Many free-flying birds escape because no one was watching at that crucial moment when a door or window was opened.

Any tips on bird-proofing my house before I let my bird out to fly around?

Bird-proof is a vague term. If your bird is chewing walls and drywall, make sure there are no places where he can perch to chew these things. If you are worried about him pooping all over the place, you need to cover things to protect them. Birds can chew electrical wires or eat lead weights from the bottoms of drapes. I have heard of many birds flying into pots of boiling soup because their owners were cooking and didn't pay attention. But if you are watching your bird, you can stop him from chewing up the walls and you can clean up if he poops on something.

You can bird-proof one room to create a safe environment, but it is almost impossible to bird-proof the whole house. Some people actually construct a bird room with marlite walls and a tile floor. The bird has perches and branches around the room, and you don't need to worry about damage to the room or hazards for the bird. If you let your bird fly around in your living space, you must monitor him. I let many birds fly around my house, but you wouldn't know it. You won't see dried bird poop, feathers, birdseed, or chewed furniture because we only let the birds out when we can monitor them. If your home is covered in bird poop and feathers, you have too many birds or too little time to watch them.

It's natural to want to share your life with your bird, but a house can be a very hazardous place for your bird. It is your responsibility as a bird keeper to make sure he is always supervised.

What kind of birdseed should I put in my backyard feeder to attract the greatest variety of birds?

There is no one birdseed mix that will accomplish this. Whenever you put out

a general birdseed mix, it usually attracts one particular type of bird and excludes others. If you want to attract a variety of birds to your backyard feeders, put out species-specific feeders and mixes. For instance, if you want to attract cardinals, chickadees, nuthatches, and titmice, put out a bird feeder with only black oil sunflower seeds. For goldfinches and house finches, put out another bird feeder with thistle seed. Generalized birdseed mixes consist of sunflower seeds, safflower seeds, buckwheat, milo, and millet, which technically should attract every bird. But if a blue jay goes to a feeder containing a mix like this, it will pick out all of the big sunflower seeds. While it's doing that, the chickadees can't get in there to get any sunflower seeds and the goldfinches can't get in there to get the thistle seeds. A generalized bird feeder like this in the back of the yard keeps less desirable birds like blue jays from going to the species-specific feeders placed closer to your house. Species-specific feeders have small perches to make it easier for small birds like chickadees to eat from them. But a determined jay or squirrel will do its best to get in there if it has no other alternative. A generalized bird feeder at the back of the yard is also good for ground-feeding birds such as song sparrows, bobwhite quail, and mourning doves, which are too shy to come close to a house. Seed spilled by blue jays, starlings, and grackles will be eaten by smaller, shyer, ground-feeding birds. Don't place this feeder too close to bushes where cats can hide. A cat can easily leap 6 feet to land on a bobwhite quail. Place bird feeders about 20 feet from cover. That's about two or three good leaps for a cat, which gives the bird plenty of warning to fly away.

My backyard bird feeder brings me great enjoyment, but for the past three weeks a Cooper's hawk has visited every day at three o'clock and eaten one of the birds I'm feeding. What can I do about this?

From the hawk's point of view, by putting seed out for passerine birds, you've created a bird feeder for him. Think of it as Animal Planet right in your backyard. I never understood why people find it fascinating to watch animals eat one another on TV but they want to call the police when it happens in their own backyard.

If you don't want the hawk to eat the smaller birds, take the bird feeder down for a week or so. The birds will stop hanging out there at predictable times, which is what the hawk is looking forward to. When it sees that the birds are gone, it will target a different backyard.

Batingo the Loyal Bird

Every bird needs stimulation and interaction, which can take many forms. Birds like different types of toys and games as well as different social encounters.

The term *imprinting* was coined by the late Austrian scientist Konrad Lorenz in the 1950s. He discovered that baby birds will imprint on the first large moving object they see because they will think it is their mother. At first, scientists thought that imprinting was irreversible and that an imprinted bird would never perceive a member of its own species as a potential mate. However, imprinting is not an exact science, and every bird seems to have individual preferences in this respect. I have seen birds that were raised totally by bird parents imprint on humans.

In the past, we believed that a bird had to be imprinted to make a good pet. But that is really not the case. A tame bird is not afraid of humans and is able to differentiate between humans and its own species. This is also called *habituated*.

An imprinted bird either thinks that it is a human or thinks that the human is a bird of its own species. When sexually mature, an imprinted bird will prefer a human as a mate. Baby birds raised in groups by a human surrogate parent sometimes grow up to be dually imprinted. They will socialize normally with humans but breed with members of their own species. However, some birds that have been imprinted only onto humans will gradually come to accept its own species if placed in a situation where this is its only social contact. Every bird is different.

In my backyard I have a demoiselle crane named Batingo. I love cranes. These graceful, elegant birds are now very rare all over the world due to habitat destruction. Twenty years ago, Batingo was given to me as a present by a gentle-

man who breeds cranes. Batingo was hopelessly imprinted on people and therefore useless to him. I thought for sure I could change Batingo's mind if he was provided with a suitable mate and left alone. I promptly bought Mrs. Batingo and put them together. She did her best to attract Batingo's affections. However, his former owner had failed to mention that Batingo was imprinted onto women. Every time he saw my wife, he commenced a courtship dance. Obviously, Batingo cannot be dually imprinted because for twenty years he has ignored Mrs. Batingo and spends most of his time gazing into the window, hoping to catch sight of my wife. This is truly a sad tale of unrequited love.

Does my budgie need a mirror and a bell? These seem to be the obligatory budgie toys—don't they like to play with anything else?

Budgies cannot hold objects in their feet like some of their larger parrot relatives can. So a budgie really cannot sit on a perch or grab a toy and hold it up to his beak to manipulate it. A budgie's play behavior consists more of knocking things about with his head and pushing them around his cage. Shiny objects like bells are very attractive to a budgie. When a bell is hung in his cage, your budgie will have a grand old time bouncing it and pushing it. In nature, budgies continuously sing into one another's faces and interact with one another's heads. Pressing his face against a shiny bell or a mirror provides a substitute for socialization with other budgies. The best toy for a budgie is another budgie. Lacking that, there is nothing wrong with a mirror and a bell. Those are the classic toys.

How is it possible for a little tiny parrot to do so much damage with his little tiny beak?

The little tiny beak was designed to rip open hard shells and husks. All parrots except for the Quaker parrot are cavity nesters and must chew through wood to expand natural tree cavities to make nests. When kept as pets, parrots don't have much of an outlet for their chewing instinct, so the dining room table may very well become the focus for that desire. It is your responsibility to keep the bird away from valuable wood furniture and provide him with wood to chew in his cage. If you don't give him wood to chew, he will find something else, which might be his feathers. People regularly bring me birds for nail and feather trimming, and I can tell if they're kept in cages with metal or plastic toys. These owners feel it is pointless to put wood toys in their bird's cage because the birds chew them up, but that's the whole point.

Once a month, I go to The Home Depot and buy 8-foot lengths of 1 x 2s and 2 x 3s. These only cost six dollars. I cut them to fit all my birds' cages. Whenever a bird chews up his perch, I replace the perch with one of these. This way, my birds always have something to chew and I don't have to keep buying twenty-dollar wooden bird toys. Don't worry that these perches are square rather than round. The bird will have it customized in no time.

What is cuttlebone? Does my bird need cuttlebone?

A cuttlebone is the skeleton of the cuttlefish, a squidlike creature that lives in the ocean. After cuttlefish spawn, they die off and decay in the ocean. Their skeletons wash up on Mediterranean beaches and are gathered and sold all over the world, often with little metal clips attached for hanging in birdcages. Cuttlebones are full of calcium and have a nice texture that caged birds enjoy chewing and pecking. However, the amount of usable calcium in a cuttlebone is quite small, so don't think that a cuttlebone is going to supply all of the calcium that your bird needs. If your vet informs you that your bird has a calcium deficiency, the best way to correct this is by providing liquid calcium in its water supply. A cuttlebone supplies insignificant nutrients, but birds should have them because they're so enjoyable and affordable.

How do I get my bird to play with his toys? He seems completely disinterested in them.

Some birds are more curious about the natural world than others. These birds will rarely play with toys, but they can learn over time. The best way to get a bird to interact with toys is by putting them in his food dish. Use small hand toys that the bird must knock about to get to his food. As time goes by, he will become comfortable picking up these toys and tossing them out of his way. At that point, tie the toys to the side of his cage with some shoelaces or little lanyards. This makes it more difficult for him to move them out of the way of his food. He must pick up and hold these objects and will eventually come to enjoy doing so. Then start moving them farther away from his food dish. In no time, he will go out of his way to hold and manipulate these objects because:

A. He associates them with the idea that food is forthcoming.

B. It's a fun thing to do.

You can also try playing with the toy in front of the bird, "showing" him that the object is fun, or placing the toy in different locations, such as near a perch, to entice him. Ultimately, however, only the bird can decide that interacting with these objects is worthwhile. You cannot reason with him and explain that he should play with a toy because you just paid ten dollars for it.

Are there any games I can play with my bird?

A fun game for birds is hide-and-seek. In nature, birds are constantly looking for food. This occupies 90 percent of their day. We put food in the bird's cage, and consequently he has a lot of time on his hands. Professional bird trainers use food rewards to teach their birds specific behaviors. For instance, if a bird needs four ounces of food per day, the trainer portions it into hourly meals that are given as training rewards. These birds are never bored.

Although I keep talking about clicker training and positive reinforcement for pet birds, I realize that most people don't have time for this. But you can still spend a half hour a day playing hide-and-seek with your bird. If he loves seeds but he isn't crazy about pellets, leave pellets in his cage when you go to work. When you come home, put your bird on the table and put a seed on the table. He will run over and grab it. The bird will run all over to grab the seeds as you place them on the table. To make it more interesting, hide a seed under a Dixie cup or a napkin. This gives him exercise, social interaction, and a fun mental challenge. Whether you have a zebra finch or a hyacinth macaw, this is what the bird would be doing in its natural habitat. A half hour of this every day will do wonders to keep your bird entertained.

How often should I play with my bird each day? Is it possible to play with him too much?

The jury is out on this one. If you talk to the angry, judgmental people on the Internet, they would have you quit your job and interact with your bird 24/7.

However, in the real world, things don't quite work that way. Some of my pet birds, such as Harry the scarlet macaw, Dante the raven, and Darwin the African Grey, go days without any interaction with me. Then I will suddenly need to do three TV shoots and we practically live together for three or four days. Once you develop a relationship with your bird, it's like the way my father used to describe his old friends. No matter how much time passed between their meetings, when they did get together, it seemed as though they'd never been separated.

A common mistake people make with a new bird is to spend all of their time with it. I have never spent a great deal of time with my birds. When they do get my attention, they appreciate it for what it is. It is important for a new bird to learn to stay in its cage and spend time on its own while people are in the same room. This can be very hard for the human family members at first. People often tell me that they want to buy a bird but plan to wait until they retire or take vacation time so they can spend lots of time with it. That's really the wrong approach. The bird should come into your household during your normal routine of school, work, and so forth. This way, the bird learns that sometimes you can give it a lot of attention, and sometimes you can't. When you can't, offer plenty of toys or foraging opportunities in the bird's cage to encourage independent play.

Birds, more than any other creatures, are able to accept random events. Just consider the birds outside. Maybe it will rain for six days straight and the birds are forced to hide in bushes, patiently waiting for the rain to stop. Then a sunny day arrives, and they take full advantage of it. Then a hurricane comes along, or a blizzard, and life goes on. Wild birds understand that life is unpredictable, and they deal with it accordingly. It's equally important for a pet bird to accept that life is full of random events. When something unpredictable happens, they can cope with it.

What is a bird club? Should I join one?

Years ago, bird clubs were mainly for people who bred and showed birds. They exchanged stories and information, and these groups functioned in a fashion similar to dog and cat clubs today. However, parrots are not bred to a particular standard like finches, cockatiels, and canaries are. Exhibiting them seems rather pointless, although many years ago I belonged to a parrot club that did hold shows. The pet parrots were judged on how closely they resembled the same species living in a wild environment. Condition and deportment are directly related to husbandry. I don't know of any bird clubs holding exhibitions like this today. Most clubs provide opportunities for bird owners to meet and exchange stories to learn from one another. Many people who keep birds are considered nutty by their friends and find it refreshing to socialize with other bird lovers.

The problem is that when a club grows, it invariably becomes a large group—different people with one common interest. They might not normally get along without that common interest. Everyone starts to argue and bicker, and the club eventually fragments. But, until that happens, bird clubs provide a nice way to meet other bird lovers. The best way to find a bird club is to look under club listings in *Bird Talk* magazine. This is probably the best bird magazine today. Years ago, *American Cage Bird* magazine was *the* bird magazine, but it folded. The nice thing about *Bird Talk* is that the editors publish information only from credible experts, which is not the case with many Internet sites. Anybody can get on the Internet and make claims about bird care and behavior with no way to substantiate their opinions. Pet people are inclined to accept Internet advice at face value, and that can be dangerous.

My Penguin Learning Experience

In 1978, I got a pair of penguins, Ping and Pong, from a man named Charles Chase in Florida. They were imported from Argentina, and I'm not sure how old they were when I got them. I used them extensively for photography work for the year that I had them, but the main reason that I got them was because I had always wanted to learn about penguins.

The first thing I learned is how hard penguins can bite. They can also slap you with their wings so hard, it leaves a big bruise on your shin. They were not easy to feed because they won't take food off the ground. For the entire time I had them, they refused to take any food that was placed on the ground or floating in their pool. I had to feed them by placing food in their beaks. In the summer, they did fine in an outdoor pool, but I didn't have an indoor pool large enough for them. That turned out to be the biggest complication. Like all fish-eating birds, their poop smells very foul because of their high-protein diet. Another problem is that the fish they eat, such as mackerel and herring, is very expensive.

They make funny noises and sound sort of like donkeys braying. But I really can't say that Ping and Pong had very much personality. That may have been because I didn't raise them from babies. I have known other people who raised their penguins from babies, and those birds turned out to have lots of personality.

My penguins always seemed to view me with a certain amount of suspicion. I have had other wild birds like loons and cormorants that reminded me of the penguins. I have found that most fish-eating birds seem to view the world with disdain and act like they know more than we do. They have a look about them that gives the impression that they are concealing highly important secrets.

I had them for a year and learned as much as I needed to know about penguins. Even though everybody loves penguins, there is surprisingly little information available about them in books. The only way to truly know them is to live with them. I finally sold Ping and Pong to a friend of mine in California who didn't have to worry about indoor pools. After they left, Ping and Pong actually bred and produced two babies. (They would not have bred here because my pool wasn't big enough for them.)

The penguin industry has actually grown quite large since I had mine. In the late 1970s and early 1980s, a lot of people started going to South America and the South Pole to collect penguin eggs. Most of the penguins you find in zoos today are from eggs that were collected. Penguin husbandry has become pretty straightforward, and almost all penguin species, even the big emperor penguins, are successfully bred in captivity these days. But I still would not recommend them as pets. If you have your heart set on a water bird, a duck makes a much better pet than a penguin does.

My Senegal parrot is an African bird. Does this have any effect on his behavior or dietary needs?

As a general rule, most African birds from the genus *Poicephalus*, like the Senegal, or the genus *Psittacus*, like the African Grey, are much quieter than birds from Indonesia or South America (neotropical birds). African parrots also need a little more calcium in their diets than neotropical birds do.

What's the difference between a parrot and a conure? It looks just like a miniature parrot to me.

All parrotlike birds that we keep are from the taxonomic order of Psittaciformes. They share some identifying characteristics such as a large head, short neck, hooked bill, zygodactyl feet (grasping foot with two toes in front and two toes behind), and a thick, fleshy area of skin at the base of the bill called cere, which is feathered in some species. Their plumage is rather sparse, with powder downs scattered throughout. These powder downs grow continuously and break off as they grow. The bird spreads this powder through its feathers to make them soft and waterproof.

Parrotlike birds also have some notable differences. Most conures are from the genus *Aratinga* or *Pyhurrha*—they have long, graduated tails and unfeathered areas around the eyes. All conures are from South America. We tend to call all of these birds parrots even though a taxonomist would beg to differ.

There is actually no such thing as a parrot per se. The order of Psittaciformes technically refers to the whole family of parrotlike birds. All birds in this family have the same beak structure, the same zygodactyl feet, and powder downs under their wing feathers, although some parrots have more than others do.

They also have features that set them apart. In other words, each bird in the parrot family has specific traits that make it a macaw, an Amazon, a conure, a parakeet, or a cockatoo. But none of these birds are "plain old parrots." For instance, an Amazon has a square tail and a small area of skin around the eyes. The African Grey has a square tail and a large area of unfeathered skin on the face. A parakeet has a long, graduated tail like a conure but has feathering all around the eyes. A macaw has a long, graduated tail and an area of unfeathered skin on the face, as does the African Grey. Each member of the parrot family can be identified by unique physical characteristics like these.

Is the African Grey really the most intelligent bird?

African Grey parrots have been kept as pets since Roman times. As a result, they have centuries of great publicity. Their intelligence has also been intensively studied. But so far these studies have been limited to only African Greys, so it's really not fair to claim that they are more intelligent than other birds until similar research has been carried out on all other species. All of my birds, even pigeons, have exhibited surprising intelligence.

The appeal of the African Grey is partly aesthetic and partly anthropomorphic. They imitate human voices, show affection, respond to flattery, and use their feet as hands. This encourages us to rate African Greys higher than, say, chickens, which we eat. If we set African Greys apart from chickens, we feel less guilty about eating chickens.

How do I tell if my bird is male or female? What's the deal with surgical sexing? It sounds like these birds are getting sex-change operations.

Many pet birds are not sexually dimorphic, and it's very hard to tell males from females in some finches, parrots, and certain soft-billed birds. Years ago, we tossed a coin or took a guess. When I was a kid, a common practice was to suspend a needle by a thread over the bird's back. If the needle swung back and forth from head to tail, it was a male. If it swung in a circle, the bird was female. It worked 50 percent of the time.

In the 1970s, veterinarians realized that they could use a laparoscope to examine birds' ovaries and testicles. This was called surgical sexing. Nowadays, we have DNA testing, which is even better. For a nominal fee, a lab can do a DNA analysis to determine your bird's sex from a few feathers or a drop of blood. You get a little card in the mail informing you of your bird's sex. Some bird breeders still prefer surgical sexing because during the procedure the vet can also check for any internal problems and determine whether the bird's ovaries or testicles are in good condition for breeding. But if you only have a pet bird, and it is important for you to know its sex, whether it's a finch or a macaw, the DNA test is easy and affordable, and it's a lot more accurate than swinging a needle over the bird.

What are some good finches to mix together that are pretty and have a nice song?

The finch with the best song is the canary, of course. But the domestication process has interfered with their social skills, and they don't really mix well. There are finches that sing very well and mix well with other birds, such as the African green singing finch, the African Grey singing finch, the Cuban melodious finch, and the Australian star finch. All of these have wonderful songs. In my mind, even the little Australian zebra finch has a very cute song. As a general rule, most finches of equal size, kept in large enough cages, will live happily together. It is easier on the group to mix male finches only. If you have both sexes and a pair decides to breed, they will do it at the expense of the other birds in the cage. Some finches, like the Gouldian finch, hardly sing at all, but their bright colors more than make up for the fact that they are nearly mute. The Gouldian finch does have a song, but it is so faint that someone like me who is hard of hearing will have difficulty hearing it.

Which variety of canary is known to be the best singer?

Some canaries are bred for looks, called type canaries. Some are bred for color, called color canaries. And some are bred for song, known as song canaries. Although any male canary will sing, song canaries will sing the best. The original song canary was the roller canary, so named for its rolling song. These were never very popular as pets because they sing with their beaks closed. This makes it hard to hear them sometimes, at least for me. The natural canary song, produced with an open beak, has more of a chopping sound. Thus canaries that sang with their beaks open became known as choppers. Back

in the 1930s, canary breeders crossed choppers and rollers to create a singing bird with a bit more volume. These were known as American singers, one of the few American canaries. Their song is very, very nice. They are bred and shown for their song. At canary shows, male American singers are kept in covered, individual cages. During judging, each cage is uncovered and the bird immediately sings. The birds are judged on the length of their song, its consistency and timing, and the quality of the notes, according to a standard devised by the canary club.

Another loud song canary is the Spanish Timbrado, which has an extremely long, chopping sound. Some people find them a bit too loud. I love the sound of any singing canary, but you cannot beat an American singer. As a bonus, they are also bred in colors from red to white to yellow and every combination in between.

I was told that my parrot is a hybrid. Is that possible?

A hybrid is a cross between two different species. Just as you cannot cross a dog and a cat, you cannot cross a macaw and a crow. They are both birds, but they are totally unrelated. You can cross a female dog and a male coyote to create a coydog, and you can cross a blue and gold macaw with a scarlet macaw to create a Catalina macaw (named such because the first crosses occurred on Catalina Island in California). Some aviculturists take issue with the idea of hybrid birds, but I think it is an important step in the domestication process.

Critics have claimed that these gene pools must remain pure because they are endangered in the wild and captive populations will be needed to replenish them. I believe this is a fallacy. It is extremely difficult for a captive-born parrot to adapt to the wild. This has been tried many times with thick-billed parrots and has failed miserably. As long as the wild bird's habitat is undisturbed, parrots will flourish. No country with native parrots wants captive-born parrots introduced into these populations because of the risk of transmitting diseases from captive to wild birds. All birds born in captivity are here to stay.

In the past, canaries were only available in yellow, white, and green. Bird fanciers hybridized them with other types of finches such as the Venezuelan red-hooded siskin, and some hybrid offspring were fertile. These fertile canary/siskin hybrids carried the gene for red color. When crossed back to domestic canaries, it introduced the red color, and selective breeding led to the creation of the red factor canary. Hybridization should not be considered a moral issue; it is just another step toward domestication.

Can you recommend a good type of bird that is not messy, noisy, or destructive? I really want a bird, but I don't want my neighbors or my roommate complaining.

Most parrots are destructive because they like to chew. They are also noisier than other birds. Doves cannot chew, but they do coo loudly, which may rule them out. Larger birds are inevitably more messy, so you should scale your search down to canaries and finches. If your roommates are really picky, don't get a male canary—they may complain about the singing. Female canaries and most finches only make little tweets. They are definitely not destructive, and their potential to make a mess depends on the number of birds you keep and the amount of freedom you give them.

If you spend time with them and train them, they are just as friendly and interactive as larger, more glamorous birds. Canaries and finches can learn to fly to your shoulder and sit on your finger, hop around your breakfast table and sample your food, and become wonderful members of your family.

What's the difference between sparrows and finches?

Taxonomically speaking, sparrows and finches both belong to the order of passerine birds, but they are really not related. They may look very similar to us,

but New World sparrows like the song sparrow are in a totally different genus from the finches we keep as pets, which are mainly Old World birds from Asia, Europe, and Australia. The common house sparrow is really related to the weaver finches of Europe and Africa. They were introduced to North America many years ago and took over the whole continent. House sparrows are sparrows in name only—they are unrelated to North American sparrows such as the song sparrow.

What's the difference between pigeons and doves?

Pigeons and doves are taxonomically the same. As a general rule, pigeons with long, graduated tails are more frequently known as doves, and pigeons with square tails are pigeons, but there are a few exceptions. Birds from the order Columbidae include both pigeons and doves. When we are referring to them disrespectfully, we call them pigeons; when talking about them in a nice way, we call them doves. Noah released a dove, not a pigeon, to find land. When a bird poops on the windowsill, it's a pigeon. People who

hate pigeons but love parrots should realize that taxonomically these are very closely related. They both produce crop milk for their babies and have fleshy ceres at the base of their bills as well as lots of powder down in their feathers, just to name a few similarities.

Pigeons have served man and died carrying messages in two world wars, so stop berating them for pooping on your car.

What kind of parrot would you recommend for a novice bird owner?

This is a tricky question. I've seen people with no previous experience in bird care do great with a very high-maintenance bird like a hyacinth macaw. Someone else might get a parakeet and two months later complain that this little bird is compromising his lifestyle. About thirty years ago, a family consisting of a father, a mother who was about nine months pregnant, and a two-year-old boy came into my store looking for a bird. They fell in love with a Moluccan cockatoo. I did my best to talk them out of it because this type of parrot is particularly high maintenance and complicated to care for. The father, who was about a foot taller and a hundred pounds heavier than me, took me aside and growled into my ear, "I want to buy a Moluccan cockatoo, so you might as well show me how to take care of it—or else." So I showed him how to care for a Moluccan cockatoo and sold them a bird, half expecting them to return it the following week.

I didn't see this family again for twenty-five years. One day, a family came into my store—a big man, his wife, a twenty-seven–year-old son about a foot taller than his father, and a daughter of about twenty-five. They had a carrier containing a Moluccan cockatoo. As it turned out, this was the same family. Shortly after buying the bird twenty-five years earlier, they had moved to

Ulterior Motives

One day, in high school, I brought a couple of my birds to class as models for a science project. To my delight, a bevy of pretty girls was fascinated by my birds, and I became the center of attention for the first time in my life! Shortly afterward, one of the more popular boys in my class—who until then wouldn't even make eye contact with me—came up to ask me about birds. He had decided to get a pet bird and wanted my advice on what kind to get. I looked at him as if he had three heads—this question was so incongruous coming from someone like him. I agreed to help him select a bird, and after some research he decided to get a cockatiel. I helped him get a baby cockatiel, and he trained it per my instructions. He became quite proficient, and eventually the bird would sit on his shoulder all day. Then he started bringing it to school, which attracted the expected attention from pretty girls. I didn't think much about this because we graduated soon after that. But, twenty-five years later, I met him at our high school reunion. He admitted that he only thought of getting a bird because of all the attention I got from girls when I brought birds to school. He figured he would have no problem getting dates if he brought a bird to school, too. Although his original motives had not been entirely honorable, he did keep that cockatiel for twenty years. However, in my opinion, he was so popular that he really didn't need the girl-attracting powers of a bird to start with. Go figure.

Arizona. They had recently returned to New York and brought the bird in to have his nails trimmed. That bird looked as good as it had the day I sold it to them twenty-five years earlier. It had been their delightful pet all that time, and still is.

Far be it from me to know which bird will work best for you. Ask yourself how a particular bird's physical characteristics will fit into your lifestyle. If you live in an apartment and noise is a factor, don't get a noisy bird. If you have family members or roommates who don't like birds, don't get a big bird that may provoke them. There is a bird to match every family and living situation. There really is no such thing as a novice pet keeper. Rather than gearing your choice to the animal's complexity of care, decide if you have the time, money, and living space to properly care for it. You can always learn more, but you cannot change your living space or your family, even though you might like to.

What is the most unusual kind of bird you ever owned?

Hummingbirds are the most unusual birds I ever owned. Everyone has heard of hummingbirds, but most people know very little about them. They are only found in North and South America. They are members of the swift family, those little brown high-flying birds that build nests in chimneys. Keeping hummingbirds is an avicultural challenge because of their complex diet. It's commonly assumed that they eat only sugar water, but they are actually insect eaters, as are all swifts. They require daily sugar, which they get from flower nectar or hummingbird feeders, to fuel their metabolism, but without insects they will die. To thrive in captivity, they require a diet of hummingbird-feeding solution and massive quantities of fruit flies and small crickets as well as daily access to natural sunlight. When properly cared for, they can actually live as long as nine years.

If you want to attract hummingbirds to your garden, a 50/50 solution of water and white cane sugar is best. The key is to keep your hummingbird feeders scrupulously clean. In high humidity, sugar water can grow various types of fungi that are harmful to the hummingbirds. Some people remove their hummingbird feeders at the end of summer because they fear that the feeders will prevent the birds from migrating. That's a fallacy. The change in daylight stimulates their instinct to migrate, not the availability of food. Actually, a hummingbird feeder can be a crucial energy source for

hummingbirds during migration. They can stop and refuel during this long, long journey. It's amazing to think that those tiny wings take them all the way to South America for the winter and back to North America in the spring.

Why are there so many breeds of pigeon? What's the point of breeding all those weird, fancy pigeons? Which one do you consider most unusual?

I love pigeons and have owned them all my life. There are many breeds of pigeon for the same reason there are many breeds of dog. Some pigeon breeds have a particular function such as racing or flying over a coop for hours on end, or tumbling through the air. Some are bred to conform to a particular shape. Many of these unusual traits began as spontaneous mutations. Someone liked a look and then stabilized the trait by breeding the mutation back to a parent, thus creating a new breed. My favorite fancy pigeon is the Jacobin, which stands tall with a giant hood of plumy feathers surrounding its head, almost obstructing its vision, like the coat of an Old English Sheepdog. I'm also a great admirer of Bokhara trumpeters because of the breeding that went into creating them. They have enormous boots on their feet and long feathers that can be 8 inches in length. Looking at a Bokhara trumpeter, it's amazing to think that it is related to the common street pigeon that people despise so much. But a Yorkshire Terrier and a wolf also share the same genetic heritage. The Yorkshire Terrier was created through selective breeding, just as the Bokhara trumpeter was created from the wild rock dove.

Why is it that pigeons drink by sticking their beaks in the water and sucking it up, but my parrot grabs a mouthful of water and tilts his head back to swallow it?

Most birds cannot swallow as we do. To drink, they must tilt their heads back to let the water run down their throats. Even big birds like ostriches drink this way. Only a few birds can drink by dipping their beaks in the water and sucking it up. This includes the pigeons and their close relative the sand grouse.

Love Me, Love My Bird

Bird keeping is typically associated with having feathers, seeds, and poop all over the house. However, it doesn't need to be this way and it shouldn't. People who keep birds in unsanitary situations not only create health hazards for themselves and their birds, but they also perpetuate a negative stereotype. I keep many birds. Martha Stewart keeps many birds. Our homes are spotless. You will not find birdseed all over the floor, chewed woodwork, or poop all over the fireplace mantle, because we are responsible pet keepers. The birds are monitored whenever they are out of their cages. All of the cages have splash guards to contain the seed, and they are cleaned daily. There is no uneaten food scattered around to attract miller moths and fruit flies.

When people come to our house, they half expect to see the place looking like a zoo. They are always surprised. But think about it. At a well-run zoo, the animals' habitats are always very clean, and the animals are in perfect condition. Keeping birds is like having a mini zoo at home, and their living situation is just as good. If a zoo has too many animals or a shortage of keepers, they reduce the animal population or get more keepers in order to keep everything well managed.

If you don't have the time to keep your home and birdcages spotlessly clean, you have too many birds. This is known as hoarding. It's not fair to the humans or the animals.

This is the biggest mistake that bird keepers make. They get too many birds. No single bird will do everything that we want from a pet. Some birds talk very well, some like to be touched, and some are beautiful to look at. It's easy to see how multiple-bird households develop as people try to enjoy every aspect of bird keeping. But only you can decide if you have too many birds. If your family and friends are complaining about your birds, they may have a point.

Remember, when guests come to your home, they are your guests. If your cockatoo is screaming excessively, rather than laughing it off and telling your guests to deal with it, be a good host and put a dark cover over the bird's cage so that he is quiet. This isn't illegal, immoral, or unethical bird care. You must find a balance between pet keeping and your family. Some people prefer animals to humans, and I sometimes feel the same way, but we all need humans, too.

Do I need to trim my bird's wing feathers to prevent him from flying away?

Trimming birds' wing feathers is a highly debated topic, similar to cropping dogs' ears or declawing cats. All of these issues are pragmatic rather than moral. People can be fanatical about wing feather trimming, and I've seen it described as a crime against God and nature. I personally never clip my birds' wing feathers. I love the fact that they can fly. I've been fascinated by bird flight since I was a little boy. But I am the pet keeper, and I can train birds to fly back to me. Anybody can use positive reinforcement to teach a bird to come on command, but it is time consuming.

What do birds think about wing feather trimming? They probably don't think about it at all. If a bird can't fly, he isn't going to consider himself a failure as a bird. He only knows that he needs to jump and walk if he can't fly. It doesn't hurt the bird except for resulting in some loss of muscle tone, which could be maintained through flapping exercises.

If you don't believe me, visit any zoo. At New York's Bronx Zoo, there are thirty beautiful flamingos in a lagoon near the café. We know that flamingos can fly and travel thousands of miles during migration. Why are these flamingos contentedly sitting on a little island in a lagoon in the Bronx? It is because, shortly after a flamingo's birth, a veterinarian surgically amputated part of one wing. This is called pinioning. As an adult, the bird can never fly. At the same zoo, you will find red-crowned cranes and other endangered birds that have also been pinioned. I am sure that a prestigious organization like the Wildlife Conservation Society would not do this procedure if it compromised these endangered birds in any way. They do this to prevent them from flying. The birds contentedly live in the zoo, perpetuating their species. And they would not be breeding if they were unhappy.

Wing feather trimming is just that; the feathers will grow back in a year. Some people can manage a flying bird in the house; others can't. I always encourage my customers to let their birds fly. But if they can't handle a flying bird, I would rather its wings were trimmed so that the bird can come out of its cage and interact. It's silly to not trim a bird's wings and then keep it confined to a cage. Feather trimming is not the end of the world. Maybe when the feathers grow back, you will be in a better position to manage a flying bird. If

The Parrot That Saved My Life

When I was a kid, my mother tolerated multiple things, including my many pets. But she drew the line when it came to keeping certain birds in the house. As a result, many of my birds lived in my backyard aviaries. This turned out to be a good thing because it allowed me to keep many more birds, including my first parrot, a Mexican red-headed Amazon named Poncho.

Back in those days, there was no such thing as wing feather trimming. We simply trained our birds to come back to us. Poncho flew free and always came back to me. He even followed me to the garden center where I worked. One day, I was out with Poncho and I stopped about a block from my house to examine an anthill. Poncho was up in a tree, patiently waiting as I sat on the ground intently observing the ants. A group of older boys noticed me doing this and decided that I made a perfect target for bullying. And they proceeded to beat me up. From his treetop perch, Poncho must have thought I was doing something or eating something that might interest him. He flew down to the ground where I was being kicked and pummeled, spread his tail feathers, and began talking, as an Amazon parrot tends to do. This was enough to scare off the bullies— they thought he was protecting me! When I got home and related this horrible story to my mother, Poncho became the first bird allowed to live in our house.

not, trim them again and try again next year. The bird doesn't care; he's not going to report you to the bird police, although some of these judgmental people on the Internet seem to think they *are* the bird police.

Does anyone ever recapture a runaway bird?

Birds usually fly away as the result of an unhappy accident when someone allows the bird out to fly around and doesn't pay attention. Then someone opens a window or door, and the bird is gone. When you find your bird 50 feet up in a tree, there is nothing you can do. In the past, he probably never flew higher than 8 or 10 feet, and now suddenly he finds himself 50 feet in the air. He is going to be pretty confused. If you are 50 feet below, crying and calling him, it isn't going to make any impression on him—unless you have trained your bird to come when called. This is not so easy to do, but it can be done the same way a dog is trained to come when called.

If you have not bothered to train your bird to come back, go ahead and try leaving his birdcage out and calling him—it can't hurt. But the best thing to do is to let everyone know he is missing immediately. Call pet shops, vets, neighbors, landscapers, anyone you can think of. If you've had no results after twenty-four hours, try a Web site like Petfinder.com that helps reunite lost pets with their owners.

If the weather is warm, your bird will probably be able to find enough to eat for two or three days. But he will start to get pretty thirsty, and if he is hungry and thirsty, he is going to start thinking that humans are usually pretty reliable for these things. The bird will probably land on someone's windowsill or porch and allow himself to be caught.

A lot of lost birds are found by landscapers' gardeners around midday. The neighborhood is usually quiet because most people are at work and school. And the bird will feel safe enough to land somewhere. If you have let everyone know that your bird is missing, you may get him back when this happens

The strangest bird recovery I know of happened to one of my customers who lost an African Grey. She advertised her lost bird for a week with no luck. One day a fisherman came into my store carrying an African Grey in a crab trap. While out fishing that

Lucky, the House Pigeon

When I was a kid, I had a beautiful black-and-white pigeon named Lucky. He was rejected by his parents because he was much smaller than his sibling. I raised him by hand and we became fast friends. He would follow me everywhere, and his main goal was to come into the house. My mother was very tolerant, but the idea of a pigeon in the house was too much for her. Lucky would sit on the roof above the back porch, waiting for the door to open, and he would zoom in at every opportunity. This went on for quite some time, until one Christmas Eve. Holidays were very important to my family. The house was decorated, and my entire extended family was there for dinner. That day, when Lucky flew into the house, he landed on a Christmas bouquet and snuggled down and sat there. He looked so pretty that my mother decided that he could stay in the house that day. And he didn't wear out his welcome by walking around and pooping everywhere. He enjoyed the warmth and the company, sitting in the bouquet. Perhaps he thought he was hiding in plain sight. That was the crowning event in Lucky's life. Pigeons live close to death, and not long after that, Lucky met a sad fate when he was killed by a hawk. I've owned some of my birds for thirty-five years, but unfortunately not all of them live that long.

morning, he noticed a flock of seagulls mobbing something floating in the water. He steered his boat closer and saw that they were attacking an African Grey parrot. Just as he got close, the parrot sank. He grabbed a net, swished it around, and got the bird out just in the nick of time. This was truly a lucky coincidence. If he had gotten there a few minutes later, no one would have ever seen this. I could tell you many stories like this, but getting your bird back is a combination of perseverance and luck.

My sister-in-law won't allow my brother to petsit my budgie. She said budgies are dirty. What should I say to allay her fears?

You can't say anything to calm her fears. Birds are indeed messy, and people have caught diseases from them in the past, although it is very rare. If she really believes this, nothing you say will convince her otherwise. To keep peace in the family, don't say anything. Board your budgie at a vet or a good pet store that boards birds. One thing I learned a long time ago is that if someone doesn't like an animal, they will come up with a million reasons to justify this. Nothing I can say will sway them, especially if there is a grain of truth to it, like in this particular case.

What temperature is too hot for my bird? Should I leave the air-conditioning on when it is supposed to be above 80 degrees Fahrenheit?

As a general rule, birds can comfortably tolerate temperatures up to 90 degrees as long as they are not in direct sun and they have plenty of fresh water. But this varies from bird to bird. African Greys suffer more from heat than other parrots do, which is odd, considering that their natural habitat, the equatorial regions of West Africa, is very hot. When a bird is in its native habitat, it chooses where it wants to be. If a bird is in a cage in a hot room, it is forced to endure that environment. Sunlight, although very good for birds, can be a killer if the bird is forced to stay in direct sun for a prolonged period. Some people like to bring their birds to the beach. Make sure you bring an umbrella and keep your bird in the shade. Bring a spray bottle to regularly mist him when he gets too hot.

When birds are hot, they pant, very much like dogs. They will stand up very straight, slick their feathers down tightly against the body, open their wings to release heat, and move their tongues up and down like a panting dog. If you see your bird doing this, *he is too hot*.

Should I take my bird outside in his cage to get some sun every day?

This is very beneficial for birds, but they must always be supervised. Never, never leave an unattended bird in the sun. Birds can die of heatstroke very easily. When basking in the sun, many birds will turn their backs toward the sun, spread their wings, and ruffle their feathers so that the sunlight hits their skin. This posture is quite different from that of a bird who is uncomfortably hot in the sun, as described above.

Many years ago, I had a wonderful toucan named Bananas. He lived in the front window of my store. In the morning, the light would shine through the window just right and Bananas would hop into the brightest patch of sunlight, spread his wings and tail, open his feathers, lay his head on the floor, open his

beak, stick out his tongue, and close his eyes to catch some rays. He willingly put himself in this compromising position in order to derive the maximum benefit from the sun.

People constantly walked by my store window, saw this expensive-looking bird lying there, and rushed in to tell me that my bird was dead. I always had to bang on the window and rouse poor Bananas out of his sun-induced coma to convince these people that I didn't have a dead bird in the window. Oddly, most people were disappointed when they learned that Bananas wasn't dead. They seemed to want to relay the terrible news that my bird had died.

Why do people recommend UV lighting for birds?

I remember when the first full-spectrum lights for birds came on the market. I was a little skeptical about them because for forty years my birds had done fine without them. One manufacturer gave me quite a few to try, which I installed in my bird room. As soon as I installed one of these lights, to my surprise, my Moluccan cockatoo Coral Ann took a long look at it, flew 10 feet onto a cage directly underneath the bulb, turned herself around, spread her wings and tail, opened her feathers, and backed right into the bulb. There was something about this bulb that Coral Ann recognized as sunlight. She obviously knew this lightbulb was different from all of the others she had seen in her twenty-five years. It may look like a regular lightbulb to you, but the birds know different. Ever since then, I have enthusiastically recommended them.

I've heard that nonstick cookware can kill my bird. What cookware is safe?

Many people consider this to be an overblown Internet myth, but it is a very real danger. If you overheat a Teflon-coated pan, the Teflon melts and forms a gas that will kill birds instantly. I've also been asked how close to the pan the bird must be for this to pose a risk. The gas forms and travels quickly, and it will permeate every room, so it doesn't matter if your bird is near or far from the kitchen when the pan overheats. The gas can still kill him. No one plans on burning a pan when they start cooking something, so there is only one way to minimize this risk. In my house, we use only stainless steel cookware.

I also want to point out that self-cleaning ovens can produce the same deadly effect, so they are equally dangerous for birds. If you keep birds, Teflon and self-cleaning ovens are two things you definitely want to avoid.

I am moving to California. Is it safe to ship my bird? As much as I love him, I would rather forgo a 3,000-mile drive to get him there.

I ship birds all over the world every day. I ship pigeons to the Persian Gulf. I send parrots to Europe, the Far East, and, oddly enough, to South America. It is very easy. When you think about it, birds have traveled with humans for centuries. They were brought to ancient Rome. Pirates sailed the Caribbean with parrots on their ships, and all of the parrots you see as pets in the United States are descended from birds imported from other countries before the 1970s.

To ship a bird, you need an International Air Transport Association-approved carrier. A small dog carrier works fine. Use nails or tacks to affix a couple of perches inside. When shipping a small bird, cover the carrier door and side vent panels with 1/2" x 1/2" wire mesh using zip ties. The bird's toes or beak will not poke through the carrier. Then attach a piece of dark cloth over the door. The bird will be calmer if there is less light, and the cloth will also keep airline employees from poking their fingers where they aren't wanted.

Affix a plastic dish to the door and fill it with some seed pellets

and apples or oranges. This will provide enough moisture for the trip. Don't put standing water in the carrier. It will splash around and get the cage wet. The best bedding is shredded paper. It is very absorbent and keeps the bird clean. Be sure to ship him on a direct flight and make sure that the airline accepts birds, because many of them don't. Some airlines require a health certificate, some don't. These guidelines apply to interstate shipment. If you plan to ship your bird internationally, you are probably better off using a professional animal-shipping company because the regulations are very complicated.

Someone gave me a white baby duck. He is now fully grown, and I am sick of taking care of him. I would like to turn him loose in the pond at a nearby park. Do you think he will be OK?

You may be sick of taking care of him, but it's your obligation to do so for the rest of his life. The white ducks we see on farms are Pekin ducks. These

descendants of the wild mallard were domesticated to be eaten. Selective breeding resulted in a duck with a much larger body and much weaker breast muscles than a wild duck would have. It is easy to tell the difference between male and female Pekin ducks. Like mallards, the males have a little curl on their tails, and the females don't. However, none of them can fly. If you leave your Pekin duck at a park pond, he may look happy as you walk away, get in your car, and drive off. But in a short time he will be eaten by a raccoon or a fox. If he manages to last until winter, when the pond freezes over the poor bird will die an even worse death. These domestic ducks raised as pets have no survival skills.

If they do not die right away, it is not unusual for male Pekin ducks to mate with female mallards, resulting in hybrid crosses that are are also unable to survive in the wild. This also damages the wild duck gene pool.

White Pekin ducks do make very nice pets, and they require very little care. A small backyard pen with a kiddie pool makes a fine habitat for a pet duck. They can live for eight or nine years when properly cared for. The Pekin duck does need a lot of calcium in its diet, though. They have much bigger, heavier leg bones than wild ducks do, and, since they can't fly, they do a lot more walking. I feed my Pekin ducks duck pellets supplemented with calcium that you can find at any pet shop.

If you really can't keep him, you are better off giving him to a traditional farmer who can give him a somewhat comfortable life and hopefully a humane death. But please don't dump your duck in the park because he will die a slow, horrible death or wreak ecological havoc on the wild duck population. Because people habitually abandon white ducks at public parks and others regularly go there to feed the ducks, these small bodies of water are home to far larger populations than they can safely support. The water becomes polluted, and during the hot summer months this gives rise to an avian illness similar to botulism. This will kill off all the ducks—both domestic and wild.

Very often, teachers hatch duck eggs in classrooms as a lesson for their students. Only do this if you are prepared to keep the ducklings when they hatch (that could be a nine-year project!). There is no mythical farm where these animals go to live out a happy life without somebody eating them. If you want to teach children about how eggs hatch, show them a movie.

My cockatiel keeps laying eggs. Should I take them away or leave them?

This is another hot topic. A chicken lays an egg every single day, and the farmer takes it away. The farmer must ensure that the chicken gets enough calcium in her diet to compensate for laying all of these eggs. Since cockatiels are equally domesticated, we should follow the same advice. In my experience, it is best to deal with the situation in the same way. When the bird lays the egg, take the egg out of the cage. Then take the bird out of the cage and give her a bath to get her mind off of brooding. Clean the bottom of the cage and remove whatever nest she has built.

The bird may lay another egg two days later. Do the same thing all over again. Don't make a big deal out of it. Most bird breeders say to leave the egg, or that the bird should be allowed to lay a clutch of eggs and sit on them for a while, but this really doesn't accomplish anything. When the eggs don't hatch, the bird will do it all over again. This is natural for birds. It's much better to accept egg laying as a normal course of events. The important thing to remember is that the bird will need daily calcium supplementation to replace that which is lost through egg laying. Allowing your hen to lay egg after egg will quickly deplete her calcium and compromise her health. You need to supplement continuously because you never know when the bird is going to lay an egg. The calcium has to be in the bird's system before the egg is laid. Fortunately, many pet shops sell liquid calcium supplements that can be added to the bird's drinking water.

You may also want to try some things to deter egg-laying behavior, such as restricting your bird's access to dark corners and reducing the amount of light to ten to twelve hours a day.

Of course, some people will disagree with my advice, but this is what I have found to work best after many years of experience with raising birds. Your bird is not going to be a very fun pet if she spends all her time in the bottom of her cage, sitting on eggs that are not going to hatch. The bird isn't very happy, either, because this situation is 150 percent unnatural.

How can I tell if my parrot is egg bound? What is the best way to prevent this? How do you treat it?

Egg binding has been discussed exhaustively by bird keepers for hundreds of years. In my experience, it occurs when the bird has a calcium deficiency and cannot lay normal eggs. The egg either has a soft shell or a rough shell. The muscles in the bird's oviduct try to push this egg out, but because the egg is abnormal, it will not pass. The bird keeps straining to pass the egg, it never comes out, and the bird dies. If you notice your bird in distress for any reason, rush her to an avian vet. Until you can get there, put a heat lamp over the bird to keep body temperature at 95 degrees. A distressed bird quickly loses body heat. Once the bird gets too cold, she will become moribund and go into an irreversible coma. If you have a female bird that has laid eggs, make sure to give her calcium every day. Veterinarians have attempted to spay birds with limited success. In the twenty years that I've seen veterinarians try to do this, the procedure has been greatly improved. I have no doubt that in the future it will be common to spay female pet birds. And this problem will be a thing of the past.

Should I band my birds? How do you do this? Is this the best way to ID my birds? What's the difference between open bands and closed bands?

Birds can be banded in two ways. When I band wild birds for the federal government, I wrap locking aluminum bands around their legs. This band says "Advise U.S. Fish and Wildlife Service" with the address in Washington, D.C., and a number that can be traced through a central database. For instance, when I band a wild bird, I record the band number, the date I caught it, and the measurements of the bird, and then I release it. If that bird is later recovered, the person who finds it notes all of this information and sends the info to Washington. This way we can determine how far the bird traveled, how much weight it gained, and so on. Once, I caught a peregrine falcon that had been banded in Greenland by a scientist in Denmark. I talked to him, and we compared notes. A peregrine falcon that I banded in New York was found in Peru. However, this tracking is possible because the registry is maintained by the federal government.

Birds as Commodities

Unfortunately for birds, some species, such as pigeons and chickens, are perceived as worthless, and some, such as parrots and macaws, are considered very valuable. Even more unfortunate is the fact that bad people will try to steal birds that are considered expensive and valuable. My birds and I have been targets of this several times. One of the worst robberies happened on February 2, 1980, when two armed men forced their way into my store at closing time and locked the door behind them. They brandished guns and demanded that I put many of my birds, including a very intelligent macaw named Viking, into boxes.

I was only eighteen at the time and very hotheaded. After I spent twenty minutes putting my beloved birds into boxes, my fear turned to anger. At that point, the robbers ordered me to put Harry, my scarlet macaw, into a box. In my youthful impulsiveness, I turned on the thief and told him that he could shoot me dead right now because there was no way I was putting Harry into a box. He paused, and I guess they decided that they had enough birds. They grabbed the boxes and left. I have had Harry ever since.

After calling the police, I went into the back room of my store and, to my shock, there was Viking sitting on top of a cage. I always assumed that he was a smart bird, and he proved this by escaping from the box and sneaking into the back room, thus outwitting the bird thieves. Shortly afterward, I gave him to my friend Alba Ballard, one of the world's greatest bird trainers. Viking quickly became the star of her bird show.

In August 2007, I was the target of another horrible bird robbery. This time, the thieves broke into my store at night and took fifty birds. The financial loss was astronomical, and the emotional loss was indescribable. To make matters worse, within minutes of my call to the police, the media descended on my store. For days, reporters from local and national media inundated me with the same questions again and again, which felt like salt on a wound. The climax came two weeks later, when Martha Stewart asked me about the robbery during her show. At that point, I started weeping on live national TV, which added humiliation to the entire horrific experience. I had hand-raised and hand-fed all of those birds, and I will always wonder what happened to them.

Breeders of pet canaries, finches, pigeons, and parrots slip solid, closed rings onto the baby birds' legs. As they grow, their feet get larger and the rings cannot be removed. The rings may be numbered, but each breeder maintains his own database of birds and numbers and keeps his own records. There is no national registry for pet birds similar to the registries that exist for dogs. Certain pigeon clubs will issue bands to their club members. If you find a racing pigeon with a band and you can locate the secretary of that club, he can look up the bird's owner. But you need to find the club and the secretary first, which isn't always that easy.

It's always a good idea have a numbered ring on your bird in case it flies away and is later recovered. This provides you with some proof of ownership, assuming that the person wants to give the bird back to you. In August 2007, I was robbed of more than fifty birds. All of those birds were banded, and I had a record of all of the band numbers. But it would be easy for the thieves to cut those bands off, and in that event how could I prove those were my birds?

Some birds are now microchipped. The problem with this method is that anyone finding the bird must then take it to a vet and have the chip scanned. If someone finds the bird and doesn't know it is microchipped, or doesn't have access to a scanner, that chip may never be detected. The leg band is the best method to ID a bird at this point, but you must be realistic about its limitations.

My zebra finches won't stop breeding. I started out with two and now I have about five hundred! Help!

You can sell the birds, give them away, or stop them from breeding. If you don't want your birds to breed, don't keep males and females together in the same cage. Zebra finches are very small and very prolific. In their native habitat of Australia, everything eats zebra finches. They need to breed quickly, starting at a very early age, in order maintain a viable population level. As soon as the babies' beaks turn from black to red and the birds start getting their adult colors, which is around three months of age, they can and will start breeding. At this point, your best bet is to separate the males and females into separate aviaries. Since zebra finches don't live that long, the population will thin out as a result of natural attrition.

A Flock of FAQs

Birds are creatures of extremes. They range in size from the ostrich, which stands 8 feet tall, to the smallest humming-birds, which are $2^1/_2$ inches long. Between these two extremes, there are more than 8,600 living species occupying every habitat in the world, from polar ice caps to deserts to rain forests to cities. Birds possess a variety of characteristics to succeed in these varying habitats and have evolved these different physical characteristics over the last 50 million years to take advantage of diverse food sources and nesting sites. For instance, there are twenty-two species of honeycreeper found only on the Hawaiian Islands. These didn't just migrate there one day. They all evolved from one type to take advantage of different food sources.

There is really only one species of domestic dog and one species of domestic cat. But these are divided into breeds. A breed is a variation of a species. Birds are divided into five main groupings—the class, the order, the family, the genus, and the species. A species is a population that can interbreed and produce fertile offspring. This is not the same as a breed. There are some breeds of bird. Canaries, chickens, and pigeons, for instance, are divided into many breeds. These have been domesticated for a long time and were produced through selective breeding. However, cockatiels have been domesticated for a long time, and they are not divided into different breeds. There are different color cockatiel varieties, but they share the same basic taxonomy of the wild cockatiels found in Australian deserts. All of the Amazon parrots kept as pets are distinct species. They may intermingle in the wild but will not voluntarily interbreed. This only happens in captivity.

Bird anatomy is fairly uniform, but different species of bird exhibit a tremendous range of colors, bill shapes and sizes, and leg and toe length. However, all birds have one trait in common: feathers. Birds are the only creatures on the planet with feathers. To me, this is the most fun and interesting fact about them.

What was the first kind of bird to become popular as a pet?

Birds of prey were probably the first birds kept by humans. Thousands of years ago, a hunter may have watched a hawk grab a rabbit, then sneaked up and caught the hawk. This was probably motivated by the same pet-keeping fascination that caused early man to keep a wolf. These animals were not viewed as something to be eaten or worn. The early pet keeper may have kept his hawk for a couple of days before turning it loose. The bird, being hungry by then, immediately grabbed another prey animal while in sight of the hunter, and the pet keeper realized that it might be possible to use a hawk for his own hunting.

Chickens were also kept by man from a very early time. The relative of the domestic chicken is the Asian jungle fowl. Most likely, these jungle fowl began hanging around human habitation sites and became somewhat tame. People discovered how tasty they were and so encouraged this. As the birds became tamer, they probably started laying eggs around the human settlements, and these were also tasty. Addtionally, the male jungle fowl would fight one another, which provided sport and entertainment for the humans.

Hawks and chickens were kept mostly for utilitarian reasons. In the northern hemisphere, passerine birds, particularly European birds like goldfinches, chaffinches, and bullfinches, were probably the first to be kept strictly as pets. These were kept by fanciers long before the canary was domesticated. When the first Europeans reached the Canary Islands, they were fascinated by the songs of the wild canaries. The tradition of bird keeping was already well established in Europe, and these explorers had great success breeding and domesticating wild canaries. Bullfinches, goldfinches, and chaffinches were popular pets but were never totally domesticated like the canary.

In South America, the Amerindian tribes have kept Amazon parrots, conures, and macaws as pets for eons. The Amerindians kept many animals, such as monkeys, capybaras, and coatis, as pets just for the pleasure of keeping them, and they were some of the world's first pet keepers. When the first Europeans reached South America, the Amerindians traded tame birds for European textiles and metal tools. These tame parrots subsequently caused a great sensation in Europe. Before then, the only pet parrots kept in Europe were Asian parakeets, such as the Indian ringneck and the Alexander ringneck, and the African Grey parrot. These birds had been kept as pets since Roman times. How and why people started keeping African Grey parrots as pets remains a mystery. There is no tradition of this in any African culture.

As you can see, bird keeping has sprung up spontaneously in many cultures all over the world, for many different reasons. This goes to show that the fascination with birds is pervasive in human culture.

Why is it so easy to hypnotize chickens? Does this work on other birds?

This is a fallacy. If you turn a chicken on its back and focus its eyes on your finger moving from side to side, it will become calm and still. But this really isn't hypnosis. The chicken is upside down, unable to move, and fixated on you. It's not a mental state; it is because of the bird's physical characteristics and lack of flexibility. Other birds that can be "hypnotized" include some birds of prey because of their natural tendency to focus on things.

What is the bird's crop for? Do all birds have this? Is it true that pigeons produce milk in their crops?

The bird's crop is a storage sack. Many birds eat very, very quickly when food is available and fill their crops with food. Throughout the day, this food travels from the crop into the true stomach. Many birds carry food back to their babies inside their crops and regurgitate it. Pigeons and, to a lesser extent, parrots and penguins can form a secretion in the crop, which they feed to newly hatched chicks. Hormones cause a thickening of the walls of the crop. As this sloughs off, the resulting curd or milk is fed to the newly hatched chicks. As the babies get older, this process stops and they begin eating regurgitated seeds instead. So this isn't really the same "milk" that mammals produce, but it is a secretion to feed newly born young in the same way that mammals produce milk for their newly born young.

Can birds watch television? My birds seem to like watching cartoons.

Since I'm not a veterinary ophthalmologist, I cannot postulate why some birds look at TV and others do not. I have a blue-fronted Amazon named Killer who definitely watches TV. When the TV is on, she will go to a spot in her cage where she can see it and will fixedly watch. Birds can discern primary colors, but I don't

think this behavior is linked to color vision. None of my other birds, including my raven Dante, the most intelligent creature I've ever had, has any interest in watching TV. No veterinarian has ever been able to give me a definitive explanation as to why some animals do this and others don't. Perhaps your bird should be watching Animal Planet instead of cartoons; he might learn more. Heckle and Jeckle are not the best role models for a bird.

I heard that you can learn about a bird's health history by examining its feathers. Is it true that every time it is sick, this leaves a band on its feathers? This sounds hard to believe.

There is a grain of truth in this. The band you are talking about is a stress mark, which is a break or pause in the growth of the feather. The feather will look normal except for a visible lighter or darker line running perpendicular to the feather shaft.

It isn't necessarily an indication of poor health. All it really means is that the bird was stressed at some point while this feather was growing. This mark can be caused by mental or physical stress. For instance, a stress mark on the wing or tail feather of a three-month-old parrot most likely occurred when the bird was moved from point A to point B at eight weeks old. This frightened the bird, the feather stopped growing for that day, and, as a result, the feather has a stress mark. This really doesn't mean anything for pet birds. Keepers of falcons and hawks do their best to make sure that their young birds don't acquire stress marks because these birds are flown so intensively. They believe that stress marks leave the feathers vulnerable to breakage. Most owners of pet birds end up clipping their birds' wings anyway, so stress marks on young parrots are really not an issue. When the bird molts at six months, those feathers will fall out and regrow normally.

Do birds really mate for life, or is this a myth?

Some birds do mate for life, but this is not love. Certain birds, such as swans, eagles, and parrots, must work closely in pairs to maintain a suitable territory for nesting. Raising their young is energy intensive. In addition, many of these species are not very common, and mates are few and far between. These birds are at an evolutionary advantage by staying together rather than expending

energy on searching for new mates every breeding season. However, it is to the pheasant's advantage to not mate for life. This doesn't imply that pheasants have different moral standards from eagles. It only means that for this species, a variety of mates works better. If a male mates with as many females as possible, he has more opportunities to perpetuate his genes. Female pheasants do not need assistance from the males to raise their chicks, and the male's presence may even be a disadvantage since he is so brightly colored and more likely to attract the attention of predators. We try to attribute human values to these natural behaviors, and this is why we perceive certain animals as nice or more worthy of kindness and attention from us.

Do birds have taste buds?

Birds don't have taste buds like we do, but they do have Herbt's corpuscles in their beaks and tongues. These Herbt's corpuscles are not quite as fine-tuned as taste buds, but they can taste certain things. This is why they love red hot peppers. It is one of the few things they can taste. Birds rely more on a food's texture to decide whether it is good.

What colors can birds see?

Any animal that has the primary colors of red, blue, and yellow in its makeup can see those colors. It would be pointless for them to have colorful feather

The Roman Legion of Hyacinth Macaws

People always ask me where I find such unusual names for my pets. I find them in all kinds of places: books, movies, foods, different cultures. For instance, in 1976, the PBS series Masterpiece Theater ran *I, Claudius*, based on the Robert Graves book. This show fascinated me, and ever since then Roman emperors have fascinated me. Around the time that show aired, I imported four hyacinth macaws from Paraguay. These were the first hyacinth macaws I ever owned, and they needed regal, dignified names. They became Cesar, Augustus, Romulus, and Remus. Cesar, Augustus, and Romulus were soon sold, but Remus turned out to be quite shy, so I held on to him. It took him about twenty years to get over his shyness, and he is now thirty-five; he may be the oldest documented macaw living.

Once he got over his shyness, Remus took part in a show I was taping on presidential pets. Teddy Roosevelt also owned a macaw, and when we taped that segment of the show, Remus flew from his perch to my shoulder, holding a tiny American flag in his beak. Just as Andy Warhol predicted, we will all get our fifteen minutes of fame, even Remus.

patterns if they could not discern these in their companions. A veterinary ophthalmologist would give you a technical explanation relating to the number of rods and cones in the bird's retina, and so on. But as a good rule of thumb, look at the colors in an animal's makeup if you want to know what colors it can see.

Is it true that you can judge a parrot's age by the color of its eyes?

It's not quite that cut-and-dried. When some parrots are young, their eyes are darker. In young African Greys, the iris is almost black, making it hard to tell the pupil from the iris. This is also true of budgies. As these two species get older, the iris lightens and shows more contrast. Amazon parrots and macaws also have darker irises as babies. However, it can take a variable amount of time for the iris to change to its adult color. This depends on the species and the individual bird. I've had six-month-old African Greys with clear irises and a ten-year-old bird with dark irises. In other parrots, such as Pionus parrots and cockatoos, there is no difference between juvenile and adult eye color.

How long do birds live?

Many birds have a much longer or shorter life span than we realize. Cockatiels, canaries, and parakeets can live well into their teens. The oldest documented cockatiel lived to thirty-five. It was owned by a Mrs. Moon in Florida, who bred the first pied and lutinos.

It's commonly believed that parrots live to be one hundred, but this is an old wives' tale. I'm sure that many people believe their birds are quite old, but this is almost impossible to document. The oldest documented bird was King Tut, a Moluccan cockatoo who spent his entire life at the San Diego Zoo and was over eighty when he died. Most large parrots live into their forties or fifties. By their thirties, they show signs of aging; most noticeably, they lose the fat deposits in their feet and their toes look very skinny. My oldest bird is Remus, a hyacinth macaw I imported from Paraguay in 1976. I believe he is the oldest documented hyacinth macaw, but if anyone has an older one, I would love to hear from you.

How do you tell a budgie's age and sex by its color?

Males and females are the same colors, so the color of the bird itself provides no clue. The color of the cere, the fleshy skin surrounding the budgie's

nostrils, does vary in color according to the bird's sex. All juvenile budgies have a pinkish-purple cere. At sexual maturity, it turns white in females, and when females are in breeding condition, it turns brown. When males become sexually mature, the cere turns bright blue, with the exception of lutino, albino, or harlequin budgies. The color mutations in those three varieties cause the cere to remain the juvenile pinkish-purple color. When an adult male budgie's reproductive organs are no longer viable, the cere turns from blue to whitish-brown. This color change can be linked to age or an underlying medical condition such as a tumor. Many people have brought older pet budgies into my store, asking why the cere has changed from blue to brown. They are always surprised when I explain the reason for this. However, some budgies retain a bright blue cere throughout their lives.

How do homing pigeons find their way home? Do they ever get lost?

A homing pigeon can get lost if it is not trained properly. It will find its way home by orienting itself to the earth's magnetic fields and learning to identify familiar landmarks. Young homing pigeons are first released from their home loft in the company of experienced adult pigeons. At first, they are only sent out for short flights. Gradually, they learn to navigate longer distances and find their home loft from different directions. In other words, they birds might be released two miles east of their home loft one day, then two miles north the next day, and so forth. Once the bird can rapidly find its way home from one direction, the distance is increased until the bird can easily navigate from many miles away. This isn't much different than robins, hummingbirds, and barn swallows returning to the same backyard every year. Those birds fly from North to South America, turn around, and come back. Yet no one thinks twice when they look out the window on a warm spring day and see a barn swallow returning to the same barn it nested in last year. I guess that homing pigeons have better press agents.

If parrots are so smart, why can't they fly back to you like hawks and falcons when you call them?

We've all heard the romantic myths about falconry, where a bird of prey swoops down from the sky to land on a trainer's fist. It seems rather odd that a hawk or falcon will do this and a pet parrot will not. In reality, any bird can be trained to do this, from a pigeon to a hummingbird. They all respond to the same positive-reinforcement training. The bird only eats when it flies to your fist. The falconer first works with the bird in an enclosed room, then works with it outside attached to a long leash called a creance. When the bird reliably flies back for food, the leash is removed.

However, this is not the main goal. The sport of falconry is hunting with a bird in a partnership. Once the hawk reliably flies back on command, the falconer takes it to public land where hunting is permitted. The hawk is turned loose and sits in a tree, watching as the hunter beats the underbrush to chase

Birds Don't Belong in School

When I was young, one of my favorite birds was a crow named Poe. As was the custom at the time, birds were not allowed in the house, so Poe was outside all day, flying loose in the neighborhood. My school wasn't far away, and I used to walk. One day, Poe must have followed me to school. He must have looked in all of the windows until he found me, because in the middle of the morning a crow began pecking at the window of our classroom. I wasn't sure how the teacher would react, so I kept quiet about recognizing the crow pecking at the window. My teacher was fascinated and opened the window. Poe came right in and said hello to everyone. The teacher gave him part of someone's lunch, which he enjoyed. Throughout all of this, I kept as quiet as a mouse in the back of the room. I got picked on enough by other kids because of my fascination with animals. When Poe had satisfied his curiosity, the teacher ushered him out the window and closed the blinds, and he flew home. Unfortunately, a few days later Poe met a horrible fate, drowning in my backyard fishpond, thus ending his formal education. I have owned many crows and ravens since then, but none of them possessed Poe's cognitive ability. Dante is very intelligent; I have trained him to do many, many things over the past twelve years. But what Poe did, he managed to do on his own. He was never trained to follow me to school. He figured this out very quickly with no help from me. He had an incredible reasoning power that could not be taught, that he was simply born with.

prey animals out from their cover. When a rabbit scurries by, the hawk will fly down and grab it. The weight of the rabbit actually anchors the bird to the ground. The falconer walks up, and they share the catch. The bird quickly learns that it has a better chance of catching prey by working in partnership with a human. Eventually, as soon as the falconer holds up his fist, the bird will fly down for a meal. This is a true hunting partnership that has gone on for thousands of years.

I personally have been a falconer for over twenty-five years, but my falconry practices are a bit different. My trained birds fly after a rabbit lure, an artificial lure on a string. This way, my birds have the opportunity to act on their natural instincts, and I can go home and look at Harvey and my other pet rabbits without feeling guilty.

These same methods can be used to train a parrot. Oddly enough, many falconers I know also keep parrots. However, they trim their parrots' wings and don't even realize that they can be trained using the same methods that they train their birds of prey with.

Why do my parrot parrot's feet have two toes in front and two toes in back, but my canary's feet have three toes in front and one toe behind?

Parrots, woodpeckers, owls, barbets, and toucans have zygodactyl feet, constructed with two toes in front and two behind. This adds stability and helps them grasp things, whether it's a parrot grasping a nut or an owl grasping a mouse. Passerine, or perching, birds range in size from tiny waxbill finches 2

inches long up to ravens, which can be 30 inches long. They all have the same foot structure, with three toes in front and one behind, with a locking tendon. The feet lock onto the perch when the bird is asleep so it doesn't fall off.

Some birds can move each leg independently in a normal walking gait. Anyone who has seen a robin walking across a lawn is familiar with this. Yet some passerine birds, like sparrows, can only hop because their legs will not move independently. This is also true of birds with zygodactyl feet. Parrots and owls can move their feet independently and walk. But toucans can only hop. I guess if I had gone to college and studied to become an ornithologist, I would be able to explain this. So, if any ornithologists read this book and can explain this, please let me know.